Innovation
is Everybody's
Business

Innovation is Everybody's Business

How to Make Yourself
Indispensable
in Today's Hypercompetitive World

ROBERT B. TUCKER

WILEY

John Wiley & Sons, Inc.

Published by John Wiley & Sons, Inc., Hoboken, New Jersey.
Published simultaneously in Canada.

For general information on our other products and services or for technical support, please
contact our Customer Care Department within the United States at (800) 762-2974, outside
the United States at (317) 572-3993 or fax (317) 572-4002.

Wiley also publishes its books in a variety of electronic formats. Some content that appears
in print may not be available in electronic books. For more information about Wiley products,
visit our web site at www.wiley.com.

Library of Congress Cataloging-in-Publication Data:

Tucker, Robert B., 1953–
    Innovation is everybody's business : how to make yourself indispensable in today's
hypercompetitive world / Robert B. Tucker.
    ISBN 978-0-470-89174-2 (cloth); ISBN 978-0-470-90493-0 (ebk); ISBN 978-0-470-90494-7
(ebk); ISBN 978-0-470-90495-4 (ebk)
    1. Creative ability in business. 2. Organizational effectiveness. 3. Organizational change.
4. Employee motivation. 5. Job security. I. Title.
    HD53.T83 2011
    658.4'063—dc22   2010018650

Printed in the United States of America

10 9 8 7 6 5 4 3 2 1

Contents

Contents

Introduction

Most books on innovation are aimed at helping organizations succeed. They focus on how to create a culture of innovation. They demonstrate how to launch breakthrough products. And they model how to establish an innovation process that drives growth and differentiation. I know this, having written a number of these books since *Winning the Innovation Game* was first published in 1986.

This book is different. This book is about you.

In a time of economic disruption, unprecedented downsizings, and the constant pressure to outsource more and more routine functions (and the employees who perform them), books offering advice on professional survival begin to seem shallow and out of touch. Their tired message: Be visible. Don't make enemies. Suck up to the boss. And work even harder.

My guess is that you are already working harder. And not one of these solutions even begins to address the issues you confront on a daily basis.

I decided to write this book after listening to the questions my audiences and clients were asking as individuals trying to cope with a world of change: How do I make myself less vulnerable and more valuable to my organization in a time of disruption? How do I "think outside the box" amidst the piles of work, endless meetings, and countless e-mails?

The unarticulated questions I began to sense were these: How do I create greater satisfaction in my working life and restore a sense of balance? And how do I navigate my career, provide for my family, and achieve security in these tumultuous times?

After delving deeply into these issues during the past eight years, my premise is this: Simply working harder will not be enough. Relying solely on your functional skills and expertise will not be enough. And even accumulating more years of experience on the job will not be enough.

The underlying issue is this: The system wants to eliminate your job. Nothing personal, you understand. Just the way it is. But you don't have to give in to anxiety.

The good news is that there is something you can do to take charge of your career if you're willing to consider it. That is what this book is about.

WHY YOUR EXPERTISE MAY NOT BE ENOUGH

Your organization employs you to perform a specific set of tasks. Your organization employs you to provide certain skills and expertise. It employs you to manage particular functions, and perhaps to oversee the work of others. Maybe you're a highly skilled technical person or an engineer. Perhaps you lead a sales team or you're a high-performing sales person earning big commissions. You've been successful at meeting those requirements. You've delivered what you are charged to deliver. You're highly competent.

How can this not be enough? If you're wondering why, as you no doubt are, ask yourself these questions:

- Is your organization facing new, potentially destabilizing, disruptive competition?
- Is senior management asking everyone to do more with fewer resources?
- Does your organization's lock on its customers seem more tenuous than ever before?

If your answers were yes to such questions, this is why your expertise may not be enough. Your specialist skills and expertise—no matter how intelligent or highly educated you are—cannot ensure your value proposition to your firm in today's hypercompetitive world.

To lower their cost of doing business, companies are transferring expertise work to other countries and companies. If a job can be "routinized," that is, reduced to a set of instructions and rules that make it step-by-step, and if a job has portability, economists tell us that that job can and probably will be outsourced.

What is left? Jobs that can't be outsourced, those relatively few positions that are impossible to do from afar, may still be secure. Job security will demand a new and rare kind of expertise. This expertise is the subject of this book.

HELP WANTED: I-SKILLS REQUIRED

The focus in this book is on helping you, the individual manager or employee, succeed by building and unleashing a new set of skills in your work and in your life. I call them Innovation Skills, or I-Skills for short.

By developing I-Skills you will be able to:

- Transform yourself from "competent employee/manager" to "sought-after, difficult to replace talent";
- Do your job more effectively and transform your work to accomplish more with less stress and boredom;
- Discover hidden opportunities to grow, get promoted, and achieve "internal fame" in your organization;
- Help your company survive and prosper in fast-changing times;
- Master new ways of working to overcome obstacles and produce results;
- Improve the value-adding contribution of your team, work group, or department;
- Bring yourself to the attention of senior management;
- Live a deeper and richer life as you have more fun in your profession;
- Become indispensible to your organization.

I realize this is a big promise. Yet the people you will meet in these pages are using their innovation skills to achieve these very objectives. And if you invest the time to build and unleash these skills, you can achieve similar results.

The message of this book is spelled out in the title: Innovation is everybody's business. Not just the folks who work in the research and development department of your organization. Not just the top leaders of your firm. Not just the marketing department. Everybody. Including you.

So this book is for you if you're a frontline customer service representative in your firm. It's for you if you're a mid-level manager in operations. It's for you if you work in a small privately held firm. It's for you if you work in the human resources department of a multinational corporation. And despite what you may have heard, you can innovate in any job, in any department, and in any organization—and you shouldn't expect a permission slip to get you started.

Innovation is about more than inventing new products and services. It's about figuring out how to add value where you are and where you work. Innovation is the act of coming up with ideas and successfully bringing them to life to solve problems and create opportunities.

Innovation is not something you must do after you get your regular work done. It's how you approach your work. And it's about discovering opportunities and taking initiative to get new projects done.

In Part 1, we'll look at the mindset (attitudes and ways of seeing the world) necessary to be an innovator at work. We'll examine the four modes of thinking, and you will be able to better understand the mode that currently dominates your thinking. We'll look at the assumptions and mistaken beliefs that many people harbor, such as, "My organization doesn't want me to be creative. They just want us to get our work done." Or, "I have a lot of ideas but I can never seem to get anybody to listen to them." In Part 1, I'll guide you through a series of questions that will help you clarify where you are and where you want to go and will explain how to adopt the innovator's mindset to rocket your career to a higher plane.

Introduction

Making yourself indispensable in an era of disruption, downsizing, and discontinuity is a journey, not a destination. It is a process of learning new skills that transform you from being a merely competent employee or manager to being a sought-after, in-demand, difficult-to-replace key player whom colleagues seek to follow.

In Part 2, we'll explore the seven fundamental I-Skills you need to master to make yourself indispensable in today's hypercompetitive world. These are:

1. You embrace the opportunity mindset in every task you work on, and in every project you are part of.
2. You are adept at assaulting assumptions: personal, organizational, and industrywide.
3. You have a passion for the end customer, whether internal or external.
4. You are able to think ahead of the curve with regard to emerging trends, threats, and opportunities.
5. You know how to fortify the idea factory and discover the ideas needed to propel your team, workgroup, and organization forward.
6. You are considered a standout collaborator by your peers and organization by virtue of the value you add on a consistent basis.
7. You are adept at building the buy-in for your ideas and enrolling others in your vision.

When I and my team of associates began researching this book, we sought solutions that would help you, our reader, become more valuable and even indispensable to your organization and to yourself. I was hearing questions that people had harbored but never quite articulated, much less found satisfactory answers for.

Yet in interviewing dozens of adept leaders, what became clear was that simply moving up the food chain where they worked was only one payoff from mastering the I-Skills. The other was that these individuals had also created their own job satisfaction. They couldn't wait to come to work. They love what they do. They pour their best selves into it and are deeply engaged and rewarded well beyond simply receiving a paycheck.

As one manager expressed it, "I've never felt such satisfaction doing my job as I do now. It's not only because I'm helping my company survive and succeed. I get to manage a really great team of people and I'm having the time of my life."

If you're ready to transform yourself and take your career and your life to the next level, you are ready to make innovation the source of your secret strength. If you're ready to lead and to contribute in a whole new way, you are ready to go to work learning and applying the skills and the tools you'll discover in this book. You were put on this earth for a purpose. This book can help you discover it . . . right where you are, right where you work, beginning right now.

PART 1

Unleashing the Indispensable You

Chapter 1

Make Innovation Your Business

Differentiating Yourself in the Age of Disruption, Downsizing, and Discontinuity

My work with organizations in more than 35 countries reveals that despite all the talk about innovation, the phenomenon is still a daunting topic to most. The individuals I survey and talk to seem to sense the need to develop new leadership aptitudes beyond their functional expertise. But they are confused about what they should do or what these skills might be.

The skills this book explores aren't taught in universities or business schools. Job descriptions barely mention them. They aren't scored in most performance reviews.

The skills we'll explore in these pages have less to do with formal education or raw intelligence than with attitude, perception, intuition, street smarts, collaboration, passion, and creativity. Taken together, they constitute a powerful new type of expertise that, once you develop it, makes you a rare and much needed contributor.

THE RISE OF INNOVATION-ADEPT LEADERS

After 23 years in the innovation field, and after interviewing 43 standout managers and contributors for this book and combing the literature, I have identified what it takes to be a successful player in this brave new business world.

What I found were established, highly respected contributors who had developed unconventional skills on top of functional and execution skills. In all of my interviews, what struck me about these contributors time and again were their reputations first and foremost for competence. They were good team players and collaborators, who delivered accurately, came in on deadline, hit their numbers, and executed consistently. All of this, plus their innovation skills, gave them the cachet of being indispensable to their organizations.

Where did they start from to work toward this exalted status? They grew where they were planted, whether in nursing, payroll or facilities management, marketing, or some newly created department. At first, they became small pockets of originality, only noticed by co-workers or the boss. But from there, they developed reputations as people who knew how to solve problems and get new things done.

Instead of the maverick social outliers portrayed as the true innovators in the media, I found humble, collaborative, and team-oriented individuals who, regardless of title or position, were quietly moving things ahead. I found people who had stepped up to the challenge and developed the aptitudes and abilities that their organizations needed but often didn't quite know how to ask for.

They had developed I-Skills: the ability to spot fresh opportunities in all the changes and upheavals in their industries, galvanize cross-functional collaboration, bust bureaucratic strangleholds, drive initiatives forward, and engage teams, departments, and co-workers. They are passionate about generating value for external and internal customers alike.

What I found were individuals who:

- Produce and implement new ways of organizing their own departments;
- Discover dramatic approaches to slashing costs;
- Integrate dissimilar cultures after a merger;
- Come up with unexpected ways of satisfying customers; and
- Develop new profit centers to replace disrupted business models.

Deeply engaged by their work, these individuals thrive amidst chaos. They enjoy exploring unfamiliar territory, exercising greater discretion based on their solid reputations, and building a broader array of skills. They have achieved what one called "a seat at the table"—senior management seeks them out and listens to them. Many of my interviewees shared something else, something deeper. As one manager expressed it, "I've got a lot of autonomy in my job and I get to work on some really neat projects. I also get to work with some really smart people that keep me on my toes. They're a lot of fun and it's something new every day. I never thought I would enjoy work the way I do now."

GET READY TO LEAD THE FUTURE

Think about your organization's leaders for just a moment. Chances are, they look at this hypercompetitive global economy and what they see is troubling. What they see in most organizations today is a stark and growing mismatch between supply and demand. There's an oversupply of highly skilled, highly competent specialists on the payroll, but an undersupply of those who can help transform the organization to meet the challenges of a vastly changing marketplace.

Your organization's leader presides over a culture designed to deliver operational excellence and execute routine functions in a more or less steady-state world. Your chief looks out upon a vast sea of employees who meet established objectives and execute according to key performance measures.

Chances are good that your organization's top leader sees only a small pool of employees with the necessary skills to stretch beyond the responsibilities of their job descriptions. These are the key people who can develop imaginative ways to add value to their organizations. These are the select few with innovation skills.

Perhaps right now you don't sense that your organization is much concerned about innovation. Perhaps you don't sense that your job or your company is in imminent danger. Your firm just turned in a decent quarter, your latest performance review was glowing, and all this talk about disruption seems remote.

But the new reality is that this could all change in an instant. Companies, even "great" ones, go from being champs to being chumps almost overnight. Somewhere out there is a disruption with your company's name on it. The steady-state world is over. And your company needs you to do more than fulfill the requirements of your job.

Your Organization Needs You to Help Invent the Future

Innovation may not even be a topic of much discussion in your company right now. Why should you care about innovation if your company doesn't? Because you can add value right now. And know this: When a crisis strikes, innovation will suddenly become Topic A. When organizations find their innovation pipeline empty and their growth prospects dismal, innovation blips back on the radar. And at that point, senior leadership will issue an all-points bulletin to find the ideas that "we can accelerate into the market, and oh, by the way, we need some 'innovator types' to lead the way. Find them."

If you have developed I-Skills, it will be your time to shine. You will see your value rise. You will be asked to contribute to new projects and to form new teams.

You have a choice to make.

You can continue to do what you do in the way you've always done it. You can hope these hurricane-force winds somehow leave you unaffected. Or you can choose to participate in an innovative way. If you're ready to explore what that way might look like in your career and in your life, you are ready to take the first action step toward skyrocketing your career forward.

WHAT'S YOUR INNOVATION QUOTIENT?

Below are the 15 dimensions that will help you assess your innovation quotient (IQ). Unlike intelligence quotient, these skills can be learned. On a piece of paper, rate yourself from 1 to 10 on how much you, your co-workers, and your boss would agree with the following statements about you. (You can download this survey from our web site at: www .innovationresource.com/iqsurvey.)

☐ I approach my job and my contribution with an opportunity mindset.

☐ I show initiative and solve problems with a can-do attitude.

☐ I see the "big picture."

☐ I constantly coax myself to think big.

☐ I volunteer to lead new initiatives and to get involved in projects having to do with the future of my organization.

☐ I try to align myself with the strategic goals of my organization's senior leadership.

☐ I engage deeply with people in my company and work to improve my collaboration skills.

☐ I have a genuine passion for serving the end user (internal or external customer).

☐ I look for ways to take on the customer's problem.

☐ I often take calculated risks.

☐ I collaborate effectively in cross-functional teams.

☐ I see through barriers and hurdles to achieve my goals.

☐ I welcome feedback and use it to grow.

☐ I am idea-oriented and constantly gather ideas to build new opportunities.

☐ I work to build a network of people who I create value for and receive value from.

☐ I sell my ideas effectively and work hard at enrolling and converting others to my vision.

My total:_____

As you completed the survey, did you consider your co-workers' perception of you, or did you answer the questions based on your self-perception? Bear in mind that it's not only about how you see yourself. It's about what you have done and what you're recognized as being capable of doing in the future.

If you scored 120 or higher, congratulations. You've developed quite a few of the I-Skills already. You can use this book to consider areas where you can encourage others to hone their innovation skills.

If you rated yourself in the 90 to 119 range, you're still ahead of most of your peers, but you've got some skill building to do if you're going to add value to your organization and turbocharge your career in the process.

If you scored below 90, take heart. Realize that these are new skills for the vast majority of people, ones they haven't had to develop to be successful in the past. Once you learn more about what they are and how to master them, you can use them in your daily work to rocket your career forward, have more fun in the process, and move up the food chain.

In the following chapter, we'll begin our exploration of these often-misunderstood aptitudes, by focusing first on what I call the I-Skill Principles.

Chapter 2

The I-Skill Principles

Innovation Is Not Something You Do After You Get Your Work Done; It's How You Approach Your Work

Anne Mulcahy, the chief executive officer (CEO) who revived Xerox after a brush with bankruptcy, was asked recently whether she looked for different qualities in job candidates than in years past.

"We look for adaptability and flexibility," she replied. "We have to change all the time. The people who really do the best are those who actually sense the need to change, and enjoy the lack of definition around their roles and what they can contribute."

Asked how she gets a sense of whether a person has that quality, she explained that Xerox now looks at a candidate's "appetite for not just vertical career ladders, but their appetite for what I call horizontal experiences, where it wasn't always just about a title or the next layer up. And there was this desire to learn new things, to kind of grab on to things that were maybe even somewhat nontraditional."

What you're going to find in this book are nontraditional skills. They will demand you learn new ways. They will require that you adopt a new mindset. But before we delve into exploring specific aptitudes, we need to define what *innovation* means. There are so many misconceptions about this word.

Innovation is the act of "coming up with ideas and bringing them to life." Anytime you come up with an idea—a big, bold, game-changing idea all the way down to "pick up the dry cleaning on the way home"—you are engaged in the innovation process. The process of innovation is to think it up, carry it out, and repeat. Even if you've picked up the dry cleaning a hundred times? Yes. Invent breakthrough idea for the company? Ditto. The formula: Think it up, bring it to life, repeat.

So how's that for bursting a big myth surrounding innovation and who can participate in the innovation game? But there's actually more to it than that, so in this chapter, we'll begin our exploration of the I-Skills by examining what I call the four I-Skill Principles. They are:

---

1. **Innovation isn't something you do after you get your work done. It's how you do your work.**

2. **Innovation is about more than inventing new products. It's about figuring out how to add value where you are.**

---

3. **You can innovate in any job, any department, or any organization.**

4. **Innovation is about taking action.**

Let's take a look at these one by one.

PRINCIPLE 1: Innovation is not something you do after you get your work done; it's how you do your work.

Innovation is about approaching your daily work and the challenges you face with an open mind and a creative, can-do attitude. It's about seeking unconventional solutions to the problems on your plate. At work, it's looking at everything you do and figuring out where you can do better, in less time, with fewer motions, in a way that adds value to both internal and external customers.

Instead of approaching a single task with the attitude "Okay, now I've got to get creative," the innovator approaches everything in life with this attitude. Instead of looking at "being creative" as something you need to do consciously, see it as something you do unconsciously, like breathing.

"In my work, you just never seem to have time to be creative," one individual contributor told me. "You're forced to be very transaction-oriented. Its go, go, go all day, every day. But I force myself to [include] creativity as part of my job. I'm always asking myself, 'Is there a more creative way to do this? Is there a better way? Can this work be eliminated?' I believe efficiency is an art. I look for time savings every day. I ask myself is this adding value? If it's not, I eliminate it."

Ordinary people "innovate" every day. They find slightly better, easier ways to accomplish some routine task. They figure out new ways to close a sale, design a clever slide, increase production, or satisfy an internal customer's request for a solution to a problem that has never come up before. The list goes on and on. And sometimes they'll notice an opportunity with great potential, which is what happened to one facilities manager.

Paulette I., a facilities manager, got the call from a new boss asking for help in transforming a division. "I was working at a large bank, supporting the head of the credit card division," she explains. "He came in wanting to create a new culture. I got inspired. I began looking at how workspace could add value to the culture. I thought long and hard about what that could mean to me as a facilities manager. I concluded it meant I needed to look out ahead, anticipate our needs in the future, and not wait for management to figure out how facilities management could help. I needed to go to them, and I did."

The basic role of facilities management is providing space for people to work in. "A lot of people in this profession leave it there," says Paulette. "We've talked for years in our professional association about being more strategic. That's often meant life-cycle management of buildings, looking for greater cost savings and green buildings. To me, being strategic means something different. It means innovating, finding new and better ways of doing things," she explains. "There are no hard and fast rules for doing what I do. Things are changing so fast that you're confronted daily with problems and situations

14

you've never faced before, and I've been doing this work for twenty years."

The same attitude of experimentation that permeates the research lab can fill every area of your thinking. It involves coming up with possibilities and putting ideas to work to solve problems and generate opportunities—for yourself, your team, your company, and your career. It's not something you do after you get your job done. It's *how* you get your job done.

PRINCIPLE 2: Innovation is about more than inventing new products; it's about figuring out how to add value where you are.

Several years ago, I was invited to deliver the keynote at the American Payroll Association annual convention in Las Vegas. Several weeks before the meeting, I asked for the names of some of their standout members to interview about the profession. That's how I met Brent Gow, who'd just been named the Payroll Person of the Year.

Brent observed candidly that the traditional payroll manager was hardly a paragon of innovation. "The joke was that the traditional payroll guy memorized everyone's Social Security number, knew the tax code like the back of his hand, and was in love with paper," he explained.

But Brent doesn't work for a traditional company. He works for Starbucks, a company that grew from 340 stores to 16,000 stores in 50 countries. Brent headed the payroll department through this period. He managed to lower payroll costs by over 50 percent during that time, while adding, in some years, as many as 100,000 new workers. How did he do it?

By making innovation his business.

"With the cost of employing people going through the roof, I asked myself at some point what could we in the payroll department do to lower costs? Turned out there was plenty. We began trying to eliminate paper entirely, move each store to self-service, and get our department out of the business of data entry. We invented metrics—green, yellow, red—to show various stores how they are doing on accuracy because the more accuracy, the less rework and the lower the cost of operating the department."

Notice how Brent isn't thinking just about efficiency. He's also concerned with effectiveness. That means considering how his department can add value to the internal customers his department serves, whether headquarters staffers or baristas at Starbucks locations worldwide.

Observe how Brent is adding value to what many might consider routine work, a dull department. And be aware of something else: All of Brent's rethinking occurred during boom times for Starbucks, when the company was fast-growing and free-flowing, a place where experience was everything, cost-cutting was a distant concern, and new stores were opening at a torrid pace.

When the Global Economic Crisis hit, everything changed. Four dollar lattes suddenly became unaffordable luxuries. McDonald's attacked with McCafés. Dunkin' Donuts began serving premium coffee. Starbucks was forced to shutter 800 stores, lay off 5,000 employees, cut $500 million in costs, offer discounts, advertise, and look for even more ways to become efficient.

Because Brent was looking ahead of the curve, he was in the right place with the right mindset to help his chief retrench and his company survive. He says, "More and more, they want me to do strategy. I've become in effect an internal consultant to Starbucks." Innovation is about more than innovating new products. It's understanding where you can add the most value where you are.

PRINCIPLE 3: You can innovate in any job, in any department, in any organization.

Many times I've heard people voice the assumption that "My company doesn't want me to be creative. They just want us to get our work done." The question isn't whether innovation is wanted and needed in your firm, it's where and when.

"As a first-year auditor, I am not encouraged to be innovative," grumbles Jonathan A., at a Big Four accounting firm in Los Angeles. "We are given large amounts of tedious work and asked to complete it as accurately and quickly as possible. They do not want us to be creative or try things our way. My peers and I often feel like we could improve the procedures, but it is discouraged. They want us to listen to directions and complete things exactly as we are told without resistance."

A lot of young workers will no doubt relate to Jonathan's lament. He's bright, ambitious, and eager to make changes. He's also in the apprentice phase of his career, so innovation is not appropriate just yet. Being a good apprentice means mastering how things are done in your organization and allowing yourself to be amazed that they work as well as they do.

Be curious when a veteran employee or manager tells you why things are done the way they are. Certainly listen to that voice in your head when you see a better way of doing something. And then channel that big-picture opportunity-spotting mindset right back into how you do your work.

In the course of our conversation, Jonathan mentioned that quite often he has to "eat hours." He explained: "Let's say I am given a work paper to complete and they budget ten hours for me to finish it. I work my ass off but it takes me twelve hours to complete. I can either book twelve hours and look inefficient or only book ten to look good. If I were to charge twelve hours on that project, my manager would question me. HR would want to know why it took me so long. I would have to write a memo explaining all the issues. It is much easier to just eat the hours."

"Are any of your first-year colleagues not having to eat hours?" I asked. "Have they figured out how to shave time while still following procedures?" Jonathan tells me that "the innovators here are the most efficient workers, cutting out unnecessary testing, discovering quicker ways to finish work papers, testing multiple things at once, etc. Innovation for you would be to figure out what they do that you don't. Ask them about their techniques, and make changes in your methods."

Certainly there are those jobs where, at first glance, innovation would seem to be nobody's business. Certainly we don't want any innovative thinking from airline pilots, right? We want them to follow the rules, conform to procedures, and get us safely to our destination.

18

But what about when the pilot is not actually flying the plane? Wouldn't he or she be able to contribute ideas for increasing safety, or cutting fuel consumption, or reducing turnaround time at airports? In the wrong context, deviating from established procedure to try out some new idea would be a serious breach of company policy. But in the right context, any job in any department in any organization can use an injection of creativity—as long as it's done in the appropriate context, at the appropriate time.

Had I not probed Jonathan's situation further, I would have come away convinced that he'd found one of them. As we continued speaking, he offered: "The firm asks that we learn to do things their way for the first few years. Once we have been promoted, we are able to try things our own way with total responsibility for our testing."

PRINCIPLE 4: Innovation is about taking action.
Nurse Sue Kinnick was in charge of tracking and reducing medical errors at the Topeka, Kansas, Veterans Hospital. Sue's research showed that medication errors—either giving the patient the wrong medicine, the incorrect dosage, or a duplicate dose—were common. One estimate was that 770,000 medication errors occurred each year in U.S. hospitals, while untold cases went unreported.

On a trip to Seattle, as a rental car agent scanned a bar code on her agreement and issued a receipt, a thought popped into Sue's head: "If they can do this with rental cars, why can't we do this with medicines?" She was so excited about the idea she almost missed her flight.

By the time she got to her office, Sue had become convinced that a hospital bar-code system had the potential to greatly reduce medical errors and save many lives. An added benefit was that it would streamline the process for delivering prescription drugs to patients. Sue and her team became passionate champions for the new method, got seed capital of $50,000 approved, built a prototype, worked with the scanner manufacturer to develop a bigger screen, and collaborated with software developers. They piloted the system on a 30-bed long-term care ward for a year and then rolled it out in the entire Topeka hospital. Soon the entire VA system converted to Sue's way.

At the Topeka hospital where Sue worked, errors involving the wrong medication or dosage have been cut by two thirds. Errors involving the wrong patient or the medication given at the wrong time have been reduced by more than 90 percent. Even though breast cancer would cut her career short, Sue continued her crusade for as long as she could. On her dying day, she told her colleagues gathered around her in the hospital to keep looking for ways to reduce medication errors and serve our veterans.

Like all of us, Sue could have had a good idea and not followed through with it. She could have blamed bureaucracy. She could have convinced herself that innovating a new method went "beyond her job description." She could have turned the idea over to someone else to pursue. But she didn't—she took action. And she overcame the obstacles and built the buy-in for her new idea and refused to take "no" for an answer.

Sue Kinnick knew that it's not enough to have a good idea. You also have to take action.

PUTTING THE FOUR I-SKILL PRINCIPLES TO WORK

You can put these four I-Skill Principles to work right away. You can become a volunteer. These principles show that innovation is a mindset, not a job title. That innovation means adding value. That innovation is possible for everyone. And that innovation is about action.

You don't need to wait for that promotion to begin developing your I-Skills. You can begin right now, in your current position. Despite the growing need for innovation-adept leaders at every level in organizations today, you are unlikely to be asked to become one. It is a role that you will have to volunteer for with skills you can hone with practice immediately where you work. Innovation is something you will choose to focus on.

Taking on Unarticulated Needs

The I-Skills are useful in addressing your organization's (or your department's or even your work group's) unarticulated needs. What organizations need—and often don't know how to obtain—are individuals who are ready with the attitudes and skills to produce positive change. Your organization needs you to:

- Step forward and create new value when all around you value is being destroyed by competitors and economic disruption;

- Serve customers in new ways and find new customers when old ones have disappeared;
- Come up with ideas and bring them to life;
- Take responsibility and calculated risks;
- Experiment and fail;
- Empower yourself to see beyond the obvious and find the opportunities amidst the crises;
- Realize that even though no organization can provide life-time employment security, the only real security comes from lifelong learning and constant improvement; and
- Discover new ways to do things, ask different questions, and speak about long-held assumptions that may no longer be true.

The first step you can take in building your I-Skills is to develop your personal innovation strategy, which I'll show you how to formulate in the next chapter.

Chapter 3

Your Personal Innovation Strategy

Four Critical Components for Making Yourself Harder to Replace

Lisa Peters was awarded the Society of Human Resource Professionals' Human Capital Manager of the Year award for her work on the highly successful merger of Bank of New York and Mellon Bank. After both banks' management teams came together to negotiate various roles and procedures, newly named chief executive officer (CEO) Robert Kelly turned immediately to Lisa and asked, "What do we do to create a single culture?" This was the beginning of a grueling but rewarding three-year integration that Peters helped lead and orchestrate. The merger was so successful that Harvard Business School did a case study.

I asked Lisa, "Would people in your organization describe you as an innovative thinker?" Her answer surprised me. She didn't think so. "I think the first thing they'd probably say is, 'She has the ability to get new things done.' And if you pressed on that, probably the next level of thinking would be, '[She] can see the big picture, can see where someone [in senior leadership] wants to go, and can put the project plan in place to get that completed.' And eventually I'm sure someone would talk about my innovative approaches to putting a team together or to getting new things done."

After my interview with Lisa, I began to notice this comment over and over again. He or she has the ability to get things done. What it said to me was: Forget those romantic portraits of lone-ranger innovators you read about in magazines. Today's indispensable person innovates in a style that is collaborative rather than maverick, embedded rather than forcing, and is known more for flawless execution than swinging for the fences. Today's innovators establish track records for getting old and familiar things done and then they build a reputation for getting new things done. It is the combination that becomes so powerful.

Execution Skills plus Innovation Skills produce indispensable value for the organization and for everyone in it who understands the blunt reality of our times.

EARN YOUR INDISPENSABILITY

When thousands of small and large accomplishments on your part add up to incredible value-added, you become indispensable to your organization, your colleagues, and your co-workers. *Webster's Dictionary* defines *indispensable* as "absolutely necessary or required."

Indispensability is the result of bringing so much unique and exceptional value to your organization that your superiors would never even think of wanting to replace you. It happens because you develop an internal reputation as an absolutely necessary player, a go-to person, an idea person, a catalyst, and, yes, as an innovative thinker. You come to mind when senior leadership wonders, "How in the world are we going to get X done?"

How do you build such a reputation? If you want to follow in the footsteps of the Lisa Peters out there, here's your first chance to take action. Map out a personal innovation strategy—a conscious, deliberate, thoughtful set of goals and actions—that you master and use in your work and your life.

A strategy is about figuring out where you want to go. And it is about figuring out how to prepare yourself to assume new responsibilities and deliver results that earn your reputation of indispensability. Nobody but you is responsible for your reputation or where you'll be in five years.

Being strategic doesn't mean you're Machiavellian. Your "hidden" agenda puts advancing the organization's goals before your own. By charting a personal innovation strategy, you will achieve your objective. In developing a strategy, you take responsibility for your innovation development just as you do for continuing education in your specialized field.

DESIGNING YOUR STRATEGY

As you read this chapter, you'll want to have some paper and a pencil handy so you can design your innovation strategy piece by piece. The difference between merely glancing at the following questions and taking the time to consider and write down your responses is the difference between, to paraphrase Mark Twain, lightning and a lightning bug. Not only will your plans become more focused, but you'll also own a record for later reference.

There are four critical components to designing your strategy:

1. **Identify where you are and where you want to go.**
2. **Learn the business side of your organization.**
3. **Understand your company's culture.**
4. **Pull it all together.**

I. IDENTIFY WHERE YOU ARE AND WHERE YOU WANT TO GO

In an age of multitasking and the tyranny of technology, it's easy to become lost in today's business. You're putting out fires fast and furiously. You're rushing from meeting to meeting. It is all too easy to convince yourself that right now it's just not possible to carve out time to think about where you want to go and how you plan to get there.

Here's your first opportunity to take action—by writing out your responses to these eight questions. They are designed to help you understand yourself, where you are in your career, and where you want to go in the future.

26

1. What Thinking Mode Are You Operating in Most of the Time?

The process of building your I-Skills starts with becoming conscious of which of four thinking modes you are operating in right now:

Defeatist Mode: Your mental state is dominated by worrying, which is a negative use of your imagination. You're thinking back to past events and replaying roads not taken. You dwell on things you "could have, should have, and would have" done. Your Idea Factory is basically shut down.

Sustainer Mode: You're merely sustaining the status quo. You go through the motions, inclined to look for the reasons an idea will never work or didn't work in the past, rather than being poised for taking action. You tend to immediately shoot down any ideas that may arise, even before they reach your conscious awareness. "Ah, that will never work," or "My boss wouldn't go for that," or "I've got way too much to do already, I can't possibly find time to do something with that," are all symptoms of the sustainer mode.

Dreamer Mode: You come up with ideas—lots of them in fact—but your attitude is wistful: "Oh, wouldn't that be awesome if we did something with that idea," says the person in this state, before drifting on to something else.

Innovator Mode: You are alert to ideas and action-oriented. You want to make dreams a reality and create results. This is a confident state of mind. Your attitude is, "Try anything and everything until something works."

This is what innovators do. The more ideas you hatch, the more concepts you grab hold of, the more ideas you act on. The more experiments you attempt, the more feedback you receive. The more "failures" you learn from and advance from, the more successes you're bound to have.

In the innovator mode you don't merely react to change; instead, you seek to foster some of it yourself. Ideas occur because you are in motion, in pursuit of a goal. Although stress, pressure, and impending deadlines do set innovation off for some people, in reality it's a flow state. You're attuned to those little sparks, those moments of brilliance when you have inspiring notions about how to handle a particular situation in a different way. You figure out how to accomplish something on your "to do" list in short order, or better yet, how not to have to do it at all!

The innovator mode is a mental state of improvisation.

2. Where Would You Really Like to Be in Five Years?

When I taught at the University of California, Los Angeles, in the 1980s, I used to pose an exercise to my students: Design an ideal day for yourself five years from now. What kind of work are you doing? What position do you hold in your company? How does your day begin? What's the view over the breakfast table? Who are your friends? What events of the day give you satisfaction? What do you do just for fun?

If you're serious about taking control of your life, start by figuring out where you want to go. Visualize and fantasize yourself into the future as you would like it to be.

Let your imagination go. How do you want life to work for you? Do you want more love in your life? More respect from professional peers? Do you want to earn a higher income? Do you yearn to make a contribution to society outside the office? Consider the totality of your life.

If you take the time to sketch out a portrait of your life on that hypothetical day, you will have examined your own goals and desires in a remarkably thorough fashion. Just by mapping out this vision of your future, you are already improving the chances that you'll realize it.

3. How Is What You are Presently Doing Helping You Build the Future You Imagined in Question 2?

In working with a wide variety of organizations across industries and continents, I find that most people don't spend much time thinking about where they want to go. Nor do they set personal goals and review them frequently to ensure that they are taking the necessary steps to achieve them.

Climbing a traditional career ladder may not be what you are after. Perhaps your own goals include achieving greater autonomy and discretion in the work you do and in the teams you lead. Maybe you want to develop a broader array of skills or, perchance, to create a new position for yourself.

Perhaps deriving a greater sense of meaning from work may be your goal.

Whirlpool manager Moises Norena expressed it well when he said: "At Whirlpool we solve people's chores; we are in the appliance business. I am excited about solving their problems because I am leaving a mark in life. I'm helping society. And when you talk with people who have gone through this [creating a new consumer product] they say 'I am excited about this because I participated in something that solved a problem and now people are using it.'"

When you have a few years of innovation experience at Whirlpool, you start to develop "internal fame." You become what they informally call an "I Hero."

"The company has no say in who [the I Heroes] are and how they get acknowledged," says Moises. "It is kind of like a vote of the people. And what's interesting about them is that they create a kind of virtuous effect because you realize that they're just like you—they're not somebody who sits at the top of the organization or is some genius. And you want to be like them and you want to be part of what they're doing. You want to get involved in innovation because of them."

4. What Is the Most Innovative Thing You've Ever Accomplished?

I asked this question in a workshop on innovative thinking for real estate industry trainers, and one man responded: "I cured myself of cancer."

What is your answer? Did you:

- Quit a job that was getting you nowhere?
- Make a risky lateral move to take on a nontraditional assignment?
- Return to school to earn a master's degree?
- Help create a new product or service for your company?
- Organize a charity drive and raise a record amount of money?

Giving serious thought to this question will reveal what you have accomplished so far. It won't, however, indicate where you can go.

5. What Is the Ratio of Ideas You've Been Able to Bring to Completion to Those You've Had to Give Up On?

Brain researcher and author Marilyn Ferguson used to say, "Our past is not our potential." To which I would add: Those who ignore their past are often hard-pressed to change the trajectory of their lives.

Successful innovators establish track records for getting familiar and even routine things done before they build a reputation for being able to. If you never try to bring an idea to fruition but content yourself to be an implementer of others' ideas, your value-added is limited. Organizational leaders need employees who can do more than bring them problems. They need their people to also bring forth solutions. But if you never stick with an idea long enough to turn it into a result, you will never receive the positive feedback that comes from such successes. Some people are stuck in dreamer mode their whole lives and wander from idea to idea, forever excited that "this will be the one." They become infatuated with ideas that are well beyond their level of experience and their ability to execute. They become frustrated that they had a fantastic idea but others were just too dense to see its potential.

That's why it's important to consider this ratio. Whenever you try to persuade others to believe in and support your ideas, the question of your track record always looms. If the issue knocks you off guard, it suggests that you're not in touch with your strengths and your weaknesses.

Don't be discouraged. Instead, try this: Write down five ideas you've come up with in recent years that became successful. Record the kinds of feedback you received from others. How did implementing each idea make you feel at the time? Record the specific pleasures of having been successful.

Then write down five ideas that didn't bear fruit. Not ideas that you merely thought about, but ones you—and your team or department—attempted to implement. These might have been goals you set at the beginning of a new year, ideas you came up with to expand your job, new directions you decided to take in your life, even cost-saving ideas or process improvements you submitted to your company's management. Why didn't they bear fruit? What did you learn about yourself in the process?

If you found it was much easier to come up with ideas that didn't achieve the intended results than ones that did, it might mean you want to rethink and retool your personal innovation process. By this I mean not only the way you generate ideas but also how you think them through, gather research, refine and test them on others, and ultimately decide to launch them or shelve them.

6. What's Your Personal Value Proposition?

When Lisa Peters got that call from her CEO asking her to be in charge of merging the Bank of New York with Mellon Bank, she was able to rise to the challenge. She was able to recruit the people she needed because she had infused a strong sense of loyalty and trust into her relationships with her colleagues, and she did this in a simple, seemingly obvious way: "I returned people's phone calls," she says. "My view is that you have to show respect for people all the time; there's no phone call you shouldn't return within 24 hours. And now what I've found is that when I call on people for help, I'm successful because people have seen through the years that I would always do the same for them."

In addition to being reliable and supportive to her colleagues, Lisa has a reputation as an outstanding collaborator. "I never take credit as an individual; I always credit the team," she says. Lisa finds that emphasizing the group identity of the team motivates people to work hard and succeed as a group. "If there's a member who isn't doing their part, you pick up their work and get it done," she explains, "because it's the final results that matter most, not just the parts that you were responsible for as an individual."

To enhance your personal value proposition, start by getting really good at what you do. If you're in finance, be exceptional at it. If you're in human resources, keep on top of all the trends. If you're in sales, make it a point to learn new selling skills, upgrade your product knowledge, and exceed your quota.

Not only must you get really good at what you do, you've got to make sure the right people know about it. Getting better at communicating your value to the company is a constant. The decision-making process of who stays and who goes comes down to two words: perceived value. Those who are contributing the most perceived value to the company will be the least likely to be asked to leave.

7. How Engaged Are You?

According to a global workforce study conducted by Towers Perrin, just 21 percent of the employees surveyed are engaged in their work, meaning they're willing to go the extra mile to help their companies succeed. Worse, 38 percent are partly to totally disengaged.

If you were asked to participate in a confidential survey on this issue, what would you say? If you are learning new things in the work you're doing, you're probably engaged. If the people in your group are interesting to you, chances are you are feeling engaged. If you are making a bigger impact, achieving greater authority, building a broader array of skills, and seeing a pathway for advancement, you are probably engaged in your work.

But if you are not engaged, you will be less inclined to do your best work. Business is a performance art. People pick up on your level of engagement fairly quickly. Engaged people emanate infectious enthusiasm. Disengaged people suck the energy out of the room. So if you find, upon reflection, that you are more disengaged than engaged, then your efforts should be directed at changing your career path. Perhaps making a lateral move, taking on a new assignment, or transferring to a different area of the company will put you on a more promising path.

8. What Is Your Innovation Style?

We are all unique individuals, with different natural tendencies, talents, and aptitudes. We all have the capacity to innovate, so the question is not whether you are capable of being an innovator. The question is really, *How* are

34

you innovative? How do you prefer to handle challenges at work?

There is no shortage of inventories and assessment tools to give you a better sense of your preferred style. The one I favor, and have used in my consulting work, is called the Innovation Styles Inventory.

Created by William Miller, a former lecturer at Stanford Business School, the Innovation Styles Inventory suggests that there are four distinct styles people are naturally inclined to:

Visioning: You like to focus on the long-term result, the way things could be but aren't now. You tend to be intuition driven and decisive, and you trust your instincts. The downside of this style is that you can tend to be unrealistic about the level of change and resistance involved in achieving a vision.

Modifying: You like to cover your bases and move forward one step at a time. You are efficient and disciplined and seek solutions by applying methods that have worked in the past. You excel at streamlining and simplifying processes. Your highest value to groups and teams is your stability and attention to detail. Yet you are at a disadvantage when there's no real history to draw from or when there's a great deal of uncertainty. In these situations, you need to team up with others in the exploring and visioning styles to expand the options. You need to remind yourself to assault your assumptions, especially when your firm is facing disruption in the marketplace.

Exploring: You tend to go off enthusiastically in new directions, without a lot of focus, and without a lot of prodding.

You are great at turning "conventional wisdom" on its head. You are the person whom a team orchestrator would be smart to invite onboard. But you chafe when the work structure is too tightly organized or when those around you want to go by the book.

Experimenting: You like facts and working models and are prone to experimentation. Your advantage is that once a common process or approach to understanding a situation is established, you can troubleshoot just about anything. Your contribution to collaborative groups is your systematic, thorough evaluation of new ideas and your uncanny ability to build consensus for practical solutions. But you can get caught up in overtesting and overanalyzing, and you lose the sense of urgency to get new things done.

These summaries are just that: condensations of different preferences. To become thoroughly familiar with your preferred style (which is often a combination of two styles), take an online survey.

Now that you've spent some time considering where you are and where you want to go, we can turn to the second critical component in designing your personal innovation strategy: analyzing your organization.

II. LEARN THE BUSINESS SIDE OF YOUR ORGANIZATION

I am constantly amazed by the number of people who have little knowledge of the business they work for. Several years ago I was ushered around a legendary Silicon Valley company by a young woman from the marketing department.

It turned out she knew very little about the company's unique culture or how it made money. She was unaware of what the business media was reporting, which was considerable. Most surprising, she didn't seem curious in the slightest to learn about such things. She guided our tour from notes she'd printed from the company's intranet.

As my father used to say, "Everybody is different." But if you're going to innovate, understanding your firm's business model and culture is a must. A business model is the basis upon which your company makes money, how it creates value for end customers, and how it captures some of that value in the form of profits.

In a world of specialization, we've all come to know more and more about less and less. So it's easy to avoid the topic of your company's business model altogether. But would-be innovators need to know how that business model is holding up, how its new products are being received, and what industry pundits are saying about the company's prospects (and possible disruptions on the horizon). Start adding to your understanding of the business side of your company on a regular basis. Try to comprehend where your company is trying to go, not just where it has been and not just where your daily duties take you.

You cannot possibly align with where your company is trying to go if you don't read your company's annual report, especially the chairperson's letter. This is where the future vision is communicated to shareholders and where you'll find clues and hints to guide your own strategy.

How viable is your company's business model in today's market? Most employees in organizations never, ever think about the end customer. They think about more immediate, transactional issues—pleasing the boss, being professional, meeting deadlines. They wonder what other people think of them, who is moving up, and who is moving out.

To break out of this mentality, take a long and wide view of what you and your department do and how it adds value to the rest of the business. Find out what's happening on the front lines with customers by developing contacts in sales and asking people outside the company their impressions of your firm and its products and services.

Start figuring out how your organization works on a deeper level. Think of yourself as an outside consultant and try to look at your company from a fresh perspective. Talk to people in other functional areas to learn their points of view. Find out what they do and how they feel about future growth potential. Doing these sorts of things will help you dig deeper into your firm's business model, develop your own point of view, and be better positioned to innovate in appropriate ways.

III. UNDERSTAND YOUR COMPANY'S CULTURE

Although the incident occurred years ago, I recall vividly leading a group of high-potential managers from a storied mobile phone manufacturer. I asked the group: "If one of your employees were to hatch an idea, would they know what to do with it?"

"I'd tell them not to waste their time," one fellow blurted out. "You're just going to beat your head against a wall."

Ironic isn't it? Somewhere along the line—and maybe this was the spot—I began to realize that there really are only a few truly innovative companies out there and that they always seemed to be "out there." Even when I coach companies that are ranked among the "25 most innovative companies in the world" in Boston Consulting Group's annual survey, I find that the people working in them don't see them that way. Instead, they see all the things about their organization and its culture that work against innovation.

There are no flawlessly innovative companies. There are only those that are somewhat less dysfunctional and bureaucratic than others and that somehow manage to deliver growth and breakthrough innovations to the market despite themselves.

Even if you work for an organization that is perceived as innovative from the outside, you may not see it that way on the inside.

In my book *Driving Growth Through Innovation*, I defined *culture* as an organization's values, beliefs, and behaviors. Culture is really an amalgamation of subtle and (sometimes not-so-subtle) cues that signal how to behave effectively in a particular environment.

Organizations exhibit a dominant culture, but they also contain microcultures: Divisions, departments, outposts, regional centers, and country headquarters. The culture is a bit different everywhere you go. The thing to keep in mind is that a firm's culture is really the collective sharing of interpretations of signals from leadership. The culture dictates what's expected, desired, and rewarded. It determines what is, and is not, acceptable behavior.

One comment I hear in my confidential client surveys goes like this: "I am excited that you are coming to our company to help us improve innovation. My concern is that it seems as if mediocrity is okay around here, yet it's dangerous to take risks. Sometimes we need to take risks. But taking risks seems to run counter to what management telegraphs to us."

Your company's culture may or may not be conducive to promoting innovation. Its reward system may be at odds with encouraging people to try something that may not work. Its hiring practices may weed out maverick personality types.

On certain days, your company's culture may seem so screwed up that its long-term prospects seem hopeless. You may be able to list, with only the slightest prodding, all the things that are wrong with your company's culture and your department's microculture. You may have tallied examples that prove your organization doesn't want innovation and therefore come to the conclusion that you should put aside all thought of sticking your neck out. But don't give in to these defeatist mode thought patterns.

Instead, take a step back and size up your culture in as objective a manner as possible. You must unleash your inner organizational behaviorist before you unleash your inner innovator. Innovation-adept leaders are in tempo with their organizations, no matter where their organization happens to be in its innovation journey, no matter how dysfunctional.

Start by understanding your company's culture. If it's bureaucratic, proceed cautiously. If there's an established innovation process to welcome your ideas, use it. Doing so will determine your strategy, and your strategy determines your behavior.

11 Ways to Understand Your Company's Culture
Ask yourself these questions, and thoughtfully record your answers:

1. What behavior does your company's culture value? Remember that "behavior that gets rewarded gets repeated." Look around at people's behavior and you'll see what your culture values. You want to get this right because it makes every bit of difference going forward in terms of how you get new stuff done.

2. If people in your company have ideas, do they know what to do with them?

3. What happens to mavericks in your organization?

4. Is mediocrity okay where you work but risk taking is not? If so, how have you let this perception of your organization influence your behavior?

5. Does your company have an organized innovation process? Does its position in the marketplace make it appear likely that innovation will become a major focus in the near future?

6. How does innovation take place in your organization and in your department and division?

7. How (and where) have you been empowered to innovate or to "be creative/innovative" at your company?

8. What happens when someone fails? What stories have you heard, and what is the impact of those stories on others' behavior?

9. Who in your organization is perceived as an innovator, a go-to person, someone in the center of the action when it comes to "getting new stuff done"?

10. How aligned with your boss's priorities are you? If your boss is mired totally in tactical execution and is

(continued)

**not innovative in the least, this has huge implications
in terms of how you innovate and how you build your
reputation and knowledge base as an innovator.**

11. **How might you rethink your job and department as a
profit center rather than as a cost?**

IV. PULL IT ALL TOGETHER

If you've thought through all the questions in this chapter and
diligently written out your answers, you've taken a giant first
step toward earning a reputation for indispensability. You've
shown that you're willing to look at tough issues in your life,
introspect, and commit to making changes in order to reap
future rewards.

Now it's time to pull these responses together in such a
way that they become a blueprint for progress.

At the outset of this chapter, I defined *strategy* as a conscious, deliberate, thoughtful set of goals and actions that
you use to guide your career forward. So here's how to take
all these answers and turn them into a strategy.

1. Make sure you are alone and undistracted, and have a
   block of uninterrupted time to devote. Go back over
   your notes. Examine your responses as if they are
   another person's so that you are as objective as possible
   to the essence of what they reveal.

2. Ask yourself questions about what your responses suggest
   to you about your past (track record, success episodes,
   etc.), present (level of engagement in your current job

and workplace, reputation for getting the job done, ability to add value), and future (where you want to be in one year, five years, etc.).

3. Think also about the business model of your organization and the kinds of disruptive competitive forces at work. Consider how the end (paying) customers are responding to your organization's value proposition and where your organization needs to innovate and adapt. Consider what your organization's culture rewards, what it truly needs from employees, and how this might alter the nature of your contribution.

4. Finally, compose a short, succinct summary memo to yourself to guide your forward movement. Set out a few goals and action steps based on your responses. For example: Where I want to be in one year is doing X. I'll achieve this goal by doing A, B, and C. Also, identify areas where you want to upgrade your value proposition to yourself and your organization.

After you've turned your responses into a list of goals and set some deadlines for reaching those goals, you're ready to dive into mastering the I-Skills, the subject of Part 2 of this book.

PART 2

The Seven Fundamental I-Skills

I-Skill #1

Embrace the Opportunity Mindset

Add Value to Every Task and Project

Growing up in rural South Carolina, my four siblings and I would sometimes pass the time playing a game called Beetle Bug.

As games go, it was simple. When we were taking a trip someplace, or even just driving into town, one of us would invariably call out, "Who wants to play Beetle Bug?" The winner was the one who spotted the most Volkswagens.

This was my first exposure to an age-old principle: When you start paying attention to something—Volkswagens, industries facing disruption, a certain customer request for something you don't currently provide—more of them mysteriously appear.

Opportunities are like that. Often they're hidden in plain sight, just waiting for somebody like you to come along, take notice, and act on them. Innovators are great noticers. They are curious. They pay attention.

I once asked Fred Smith where he got the idea to start FedEx. He said, "I noticed businesspeople showing up at our jet refurbishment business at the Little Rock airport, asking us if they could charter one of our planes to get a package somewhere in a hurry. There was no better way for them to do it back then."

Donald Schoendorfer, an engineer with a medical technology firm in Orange County, California, noticed a man hobbling across the road in front of the tour bus he was riding in while on a church trip to Morocco. "I couldn't get it out of my mind," Schoendorfer recalled. "On this trip I had noticed a number of people who were too poor to afford crutches." Back home in California, Don began experimenting in his garage with how to build the world's lowest-cost wheelchair, and since then, his charity, Free Wheelchair Mission, has helped over one million people with disabilities achieve mobility.

Noticing is essential to opportunity discovery. So why don't we all notice? Because we're so busy feeding the problems, we starve the opportunities.

What would it look like if you did the reverse? When you do this on purpose, you embrace what I call the opportunity mindset. You make it a point to notice not only what is but what could be.

In opportunity mode, you are curious. You want to dive in and dig deeper and figure out what makes this or that tick. You might start a conversation with someone in another area of the company, asking questions to pick up some useful tidbits. Then you talk to people in other functional areas and

48

view the organization in total. You find out what colleagues do and what they think about the business, its customers, and how changes in the marketplace and wider world are likely to affect the organization. You attend the reception at the conference and reach out to people you don't know and engage them in questions.

In doing these things, you will discover opportunities. What could be a better way to get something done? What's another alternative to the choices before you?

When you view the world with an opportunity mindset, you not only see what others see, you will begin to think what others are not thinking.

SEVEN WAYS TO ACTIVATE YOUR OPPORTUNITY MINDSET

If you don't already find yourself exhibiting an opportunity mindset, here are seven ways to activate this important I-Skill.

---

1. **Learn to consciously shift your perspective.**
2. **Think small.**
3. **Listen for "there's got to be a better way" mutterings.**
4. **Pay attention to happy accidents.**
5. **Look for problems customers have that aren't being solved.**
6. **Look for opportunities to eliminate non-value-adding work.**
7. **Think big.**

Let's explore these one by one.

1. Learn to Consciously Shift Your Perspective

My friend Mark Sanborn, the motivational speaker and author of the bestselling book *The Fred Factor*, travels more than 150,000 miles a year. I asked him how he refreshes his attitude while slogging through so many airports each year.

"Being on the road is actually the easy part," he told me. "It's being in the office that sometimes gets to me." He admitted how he began to feel annoyed by all the interruptions when he had just enough time to dig out from the previous trip before gearing up for the next one.

Every time the phone would ring, every time he was asked to send this or do that for a client or fan or colleague, he would start to get in a huff. Then one day he thought, "What if I shifted my perspective?" So he put the words "obligation or opportunity?" on a sticky note beside his phone. This helped him pick up the phone with an attitude of service, gratitude, and positive expectancy.

When Mark wrote the words "obligation or opportunity?" on a sticky note, he was consciously shifting his perspective. When the phone rings and he glances at that message, he is reinforcing the choice before him. When you and I choose to shift from obligation to opportunity, all kinds of positive things start happening. Possibilities suddenly arise out of thin air. New ways to generate value for the boss or the shareholders or the senior team begin to occur with greater frequency. You develop a reputation for opportunity creation.

As an innovation coach, my goal is to introduce powerful tools and techniques to help people consciously shift out of the defeatist mode, sustainer mode, or dreamer mode and into the innovator mode.

My colleague Joyce Wycoff, who sometimes partners with me on large consulting projects, is constantly coming up with new tools to help people shift. One of her favorite techniques is called WIBGI, which stands for "wouldn't it be great if . . . ?" For instance, "Wouldn't it be great if we could eliminate this source of customer complaints once and for all?" Joyce and I invite people to think about a customer irritant, task, policy, product, or procedure. We use WIBGI to invite the group to figure out how to do it in an unexpected way.

When we successfully shift perspective, we realize that doing this is a matter of habit. And, as opportunities begin to appear, we realize the power of doing so in our work and in our lives. Somebody in a group I was working with not long ago said they have started having "all things considered meetings." Instead of everybody showing up to run through an agenda, they'll have unstructured gatherings where people can bring ideas to share. They'll pose open-ended questions such as, "How could we run this department differently?" or "Where might we find cost-savings ideas?"

To shift perspective, challenge yourself to come up with solutions. For instance, ask, "What are 10 ways to address a certain problem?" Or come up with 10 reasons why you're happy to be alive.

2. Think Small

During the preparation phase of an assignment, my client will often say something like, "You should know that our people think of innovation as the big stuff—breakthrough products and business models and quantum leap process innovations. What we'd really like you to get across to them is that we need them to look for the little stuff too—opportunities in the work they do every single day."

My response: "Gladly."

Adopting the opportunity mindset is not only about discovering the big stuff. It's also about finding opportunities day to day.

University of Massachusetts professor Alan Robinson watched in amazement as a receptionist at an Ohio industrial company was awarded Innovator of the Year. After the ceremony, he asked her how she had come up with so many ideas.

"Simple," she explained. "Customers call us all day long, and sometimes they are unhappy about something we did, or failed to do. Instead of getting defensive, I look at it as an opportunity. They tell me what we did to make them unhappy, and then I ask my favorite question."

"What's that?" Professor Robinson wanted to know.

"I ask them what we should do to fix the problem so it never occurs again. And they're more than happy to tell me. All I did was write up their suggestions and submit them to our New Ideas Program and that's how I got the award."

Start by identifying opportunities right where you are—the smaller, the better. Seek opportunities to improve how you get your work done. Build your reputation by producing tangible results for your boss, your department, and yourself.

Activating the opportunity mindset starts with debunking all the excuses about why you can't contribute value. Take a fresh look at the problems and issues right in front of you. Be the one with a solution when your unit is in a pinch. Begin to:

1. Think small to anchor the mindset. Talk back to the mental excuses that surface when we're in the defeatist mode or sustainer mode of thought.
2. Identify places in your work where you can suggest an improvement, particularly places where you can add value to your boss, your department, and your team.
3. Look for tasks that you can do better than they are being done now and ask your boss for the challenge.
4. Make it a practice to get better at whatever your boss is not good at.

3. Listen for "There's Got to Be a Better Way" Mutterings

Several years ago, I bought a motorbike to zip back and forth to my office, which is five minutes away from my house. I went down to the Department of Motor Vehicles to obtain a motorcycle license. As I waited in line, I noticed that every so often a burly, baritone-voiced clerk behind the counter would walk over to yell at people. "Hey, get out of there and fill out your forms someplace else. That's the test-taking area!"

When it was my turn, this clerk happened to be the one to assist me. "I noticed that you have to keep kicking people out of there," I commented. "I bet if you put a warning sign at the entrance to the testing area, you wouldn't have to yell so often."

He gave me a look. "Yeah, well," he muttered, "they want us to patrol that area." In other words, "I'm just operating in defeatist mode here. I'm not allowed to think or to suggest changes." But no doubt at some point a little voice must have sounded off in his head that said, "There's got to be a better way."

For every little aggravation like that, there's often a simple solution—but only if we are willing to take initiative and do something about it.

Tune in to those occasions when that little voice in your head mutters, "There's got to be a better way." That's your opportunity mindset alerting you that something important is happening. A better way is about to be born, if only you will stop and think.

4. Pay Attention to Happy Accidents

James Schlatter, a chemist at G.D. Searle Company, was working on producing an anti-ulcer drug, mixing dipeptides and amino acids in a lab. Upon licking his finger to pick up a piece of paper in the lab one day, Schlatter discovered a delightfully sweet flavor that led him to the development of the artificial sweetener aspartame (NutraSweet or Equal).

3M researcher Patsy Sherman accidently dropped a glass bottle in the lab, splashing her shoes with chemicals. Later that day, she took a hike and got her canvas shoes muddy. But she noticed that the spot where the chemicals had landed on her shoe wicked dirt and stayed clean. She set forth to figure out the precise chemicals that had these properties, and the result was Scotchgard, the popular fabric- and upholstery-protecting product.

Pfizer's Viagra was originally intended to be a treatment for heart disease. Researchers at Pfizer were trying to stimulate receptors in the heart. They ended up stimulating receptors elsewhere in the male anatomy. The result was a break-through drug that stimulated billions of dollars in revenue for the company.

Although you may not invent the next world-changing food ingredient or wonder drug, pay attention to the happy accidents in your life. Notice how serendipity or chance meetings often lead to new friendships, unexpected connections, and cool ideas.

5. Look for Problems Customers Have That Aren't Being Solved

Clayton Christensen, professor at Harvard Business School and author of the bestselling book *The Innovator's Dilemma*, urges opportunity seekers to pay attention to what's going on around them. His advice: Look for problems people have that they aren't solving very well. And there you will often find incredible opportunity.

Sam Stern, coauthor of *Corporate Creativity*, provides an excellent example. Years ago, he taught a special course at Harvard and was about to leave for a trip abroad before returning home to Oregon. Wanting to deposit his paycheck in his local bank in Oregon to cover his mortgage, he thought the easiest way was to go to a nearby branch of the bank that had issued the check and have them wire it to his bank.

"Sorry, we can't send a wire until this check clears," he was told. When he pointed out that, since the check was from their bank, they could easily determine whether there were sufficient funds in the account, the teller said, "I don't think we can do that. Let me ask my manager."

After a time she returned, reporting that it would not be possible since he did not have an account at the bank. "I didn't have an account with them," Stern recalled, "but I was willing to pay a fee to have the money sent."

"We only send wire transfers for customers."

Stern thought for a moment. "Actually, I'd like to open an account," he said.

"Okay," she said, and she began following the established procedure for opening a new account: What type of checks did he want? Did he want an ATM card or a bank credit card? And so on. He told her that he didn't need any checks, didn't want bank cards, or anything else. After he completed the necessary forms, he opened an account with his paycheck and said, "Now I'd like to send a wire transfer."

Again, following established procedure, she asked where he would like to send the transfer and how much money he would like to send. Stern gave her the name of his bank in Oregon and said that he would like to send the entire balance of his newly opened account. After completing the forms for the electronic transfer, he then told her that he wanted to close his account. Okay, she said, pulling out the necessary forms to begin the procedure for closing an account.

"When at last we were done, she said to me, 'You know something? No one has ever done that before,'" Stern recalls.

Of course, a business can't be all things to all people. And employees must conform to company policy. But if this teller and her manager had been trained in innovation skills, the bank's inability to solve Stern's problem could have pointed to a new opportunity. Instead of "innovating" new fees that are hidden, charging a fee for performing this service for Stern and other noncustomers like him could have become a new revenue source for the bank.

How much demand might there be for such a service? Could the bank make money off this idea? How would the bank know if all it does is repeat the words "no can do" to the customer.

It's common in our hurry-up world to ignore such a "customer rub," in which we fail to meet a customer's needs. But Christensen's advice to look for poorly solved or unsolved problems alerts us to the need to pay attention to such incidents and see the potential that others miss.

6. Look for Opportunities to Eliminate Non-Value-Adding Work

A group of IBM innovation champions from all over the world gathered in Austin, Texas, not long ago. One participant shared with us how IBM Japan started Work Elimination Campaigns. People's eyes lit up: Now there's a cool idea, they seemed to be saying.

The idea behind these campaigns is that there's no end to adding things that require more work to complete. But unless they become equally creative about eliminating non-value-added work, like tasks and reports that are no longer essential, it all becomes so much busywork.

I asked Matt Carothers, a leading information technology maven at Cox Communications, what the source of his creativity was. His answer surprised me.

57

"I hold laziness to be an engineer's highest virtue," he responded, with a grin. "If not for lazy people looking for easier ways to perform unpleasant and repetitive tasks, we'd never make any progress."

As an example, Matt cited how his department works with network abuse complaints. They receive around 70,000 e-mails every month reporting that the company's high-speed Internet customers have violated their Acceptable Use Policy in some way, such as sending spam or viruses.

"No truly lazy person could stay happy poring over all those e-mails," Matt explained. "So I wrote a computer program to do it for us. It reads each message, identifies the subscriber, checks for prior offenses, and either takes action on its own or provides enough information for a human being to make an easy decision. Eighty to ninety percent of the e-mails now require no human intervention at all. And the rest only require a couple of mouse clicks in a web interface.

"Most of my work boils down to automating tedious processes, so it's a simple matter of asking people what they hate to do or what we spend the most money on. I don't just ask, 'What are we doing?' but also, 'Why are we doing it that way?' Once I find something inefficient, monotonous, or expensive, I look for ways to streamline or eliminate it entirely."

Matt makes his own tendency to get bored quickly work for him. Opportunity spotting is his business. He loves what he does because he gets plenty of strokes from co-workers and upper management. By doing what he does, everybody wins.

Rest assured that your firm genuinely wants to cut out non-value-adding work, if only it knew how. It is difficult for management to identify all the unnecessary work that its associates do without looking at the assumptions surrounding the particular policy, process, or procedure. That's where opportunity spotting comes into play. If you identify a meaningless task, take action.

Recommend an alternative solution or outright elimination. Be prepared for push back and expect comments such as, "But this is the way we've always done it," or "We do it this way because . . ." Building the buy-in for even simple work elimination will give you experience using and honing your I-Skills. And reducing future wasted effort will be worth the struggle.

7. Think Big

Have you heard the story of the three bricklayers? It's become a parable, having been told so many times. It goes like this:

Once there were three bricklayers busily doing their jobs, when a man out for a walk paused and asked each what they were up to.

The first man was annoyed by the question. "Can't you see, buddy, I'm laying bricks. I'm making bucks."

The second man replied, "I'm putting up a wall."

The third man paused, and almost seemed to close his eyes, as if to envision something in his mind's eye. "I'm building a cathedral," he said with obvious pride.

It's an old story, but it survives because it makes a point about the size of our thinking. It is not the size of our brains or IQs that counts, but the size of our thinking. All of us, more than we realize or recognize, are products of the thinking around us. And much of this thinking is small, petty, unproductive, and negative. "I'm just laying bricks," it teaches us.

The innovator rejects this sort of thinking. The innovator looks at things not as they are, but as the cathedral they can be. At times our focus must be on the immediate task at hand. But thinking big can reveal hidden potential in even the most mundane work. Big breaks don't come along every day. But when they do, if you're ready, they can alter the course of your career because you're prepared to seize the moment.

TOM DOLAN'S BIG MOMENT

Tom Dolan had such a moment. Earlier in this decade, his company, Xerox, was facing hurricane-strength disruption, and the company's very survival was at stake. Tom wondered what he could do to help.

"My background was in sales, so I was in front of customers all the time," Tom told me. "I noticed how the market was shifting. I saw that companies didn't want to spend so much on documents, how they wanted reduce the number of suppliers. I noticed how companies were beginning to want turnkey solutions. They didn't want you to just drop off your product on their loading docks; they wanted help in showing them how to use the products to become more productive.

"What I also saw was how they wanted us to provide global solutions to their global operations. At the time we were international, but we didn't act global. All our geographies were doing their own thing, and it wasn't helping the customer. I saw that if we could come up with a solution that addressed all these issues, we'd have something that added value to the customer."

Thinking big, Tom went to his boss, Ann Mulcahy, then president and later chief executive officer (CEO) of the company. "I want to do research on how we might tap this growing desire for document services as opposed to selling copiers," he told her. "I believe we are losing our edge because we are not connected as a company. We need to become a document management services company rather than just a copier company. If we combine our seven business units to deliver on that, I think we can enlarge the market substantially. It could even be a game changer, the way it was for IBM."

Mulcahy was intrigued. She too was hearing from customers about how out of step Xerox had become. "Figure it out," she told Tom. "And let's have you present this to the senior team."

In his 30 years with the company, Tom had already identified himself as an unconventional manager. For one thing, he'd given up a successful career in sales at Xerox to work in the product group. Such "boundary crossing" was almost unheard of at the time. "A lot of my peers looked at me like I had three heads," he recalls.

He knew a lot about the company, including its margins and carrying costs, as well as all the hidden but necessary metrics that formed the foundation of Xerox's business model. He'd already held a number of managerial and executive roles. He knew how to recruit and lead an effective collaborative team, which he was now doing. Together, they dove into five months of intense research about his questions.

When he and his 15 colleagues came forward with the radical idea to form Xerox Global Services, they'd had

61

numerous conversations with people inside and outside the company. Tom and his team were prepared with facts, figures, and evidence to build their case. Finally the day came for the pitch.

"One thing we had to fight was the fact the senior team was composed of people who had a strong product focus," Tom recalled. "We emphasized that this new strategy was not in place of our great products. It was about growing new businesses and making the ones we already were in more successful. Finally, after hours of spirited discussion, when we walked out of that room we had the order. We flew back to Rochester and headed over to a local pub to celebrate. And the next day we all had the same realization: We got the order, now what? We knew it wouldn't be easy what we had signed on to do. We knew there'd be resistance."

When I asked Tom about the results, he spoke of Kickoff Day in 2003. "We had all the sales reps gathered together and we asked, 'How many of you are working on million-dollar orders?'" Three hands went up. "Last year we asked that same question and over a hundred reps had turned in deals worth over a million. By taking on our customers' document management challenges, we've grown the business. Xerox and its competitors are seeing strong demand for consulting services that show companies how to eliminate desktop printers and get workers to share multifunction devices that copy, fax, and print, which can reduce printing costs up to 30 percent."

Tom Dolan stared down a major disruption threatening the very life of his company and didn't flinch. Nor did he try to pass the buck to someone else. He saw how Xerox had gotten out of step with customer needs, and he accepted the will of the market. He thought big and challenged his assumptions. And then he built the buy-in for a new way of doing business at Xerox.

Tom Dolan exemplifies the opportunity mindset.

HOW TO MASTER THIS I-SKILL

Forget about waiting and hoping that someone will bring you an opportunity that will boost your career, make work fun, or improve your results. Turn your mind inside out to discover the opportunities that are right there in front of you—hidden in plain sight.

No matter what kind of work you do, no matter where you are in your career, you have the ability to transform your work every single day. You can play your part in building a cathedral, or you can simply choose to look at what you do as laying bricks. So take action: look for ways to shift your perspective and your attitude. Think small to apply the opportunity mindset to your "things to do list." Listen up the next time somebody mutters the words "there's got to be a better way to do this" and see what solutions occur. Look for ways to do away with non-value-adding work. And above all, at various times during the day, take a step back and say to yourself, "What's the big picture here that I am missing?"

If you do these things daily, if you activate and exercise your opportunity mindset to the fullest, you will look back before long and say, "That didn't exist until we came along and made it so."

I-Skill #2

Become an Assumption Assaulter

Blast Away at Personal, Organizational, and Industry Notions that Block Progress

My wife and I are lounging by the pool at the Hyatt Regency in Maui. It is late morning, and a gentle breeze wafts over the sunbathers and stirs the fronds of palm trees high above. Around me I see wall to wall human rotisseries all oiled up and turning at their leisure. Beams of sunlight illuminate the pool as waves crash just beyond the boardwalk. I watch servers in clean white sneakers puttering around with little trays, serving mai tais and piña coladas. There's even the faint aroma of plumeria in the air, and nothing smells better. What a peaceful scene.

Finally, when I can't stand lying in the sun any longer, I strike up a conversation with "Victor," a young man from

Kenya who tells me he runs the hotel's children's program. Hyatt invented Camp Hyatt and pioneered transforming child care service into something really fun for kids ages 3 to 12. And Victor, as I soon discover, is an innovator in making the Camp Hyatt experience come alive for his guests.

"People have a lot of choices of where they'll stay, where they'll spend their money," Victor tells me, with an air of authority. "We want to provide the best experience to keep them coming back, so we keep making changes to make it even better." I might have expected to hear such sentiments from the hotel's general manager or from a seminar leader in one of the ballrooms nearby, but not from the manager of Camp Hyatt.

Victor is passionate about his work, and it shows. His camp gives kids the opportunity to do more than watch videos, eat hot dogs, and swim for hours until their fingers start to wrinkle. Instead, they get to make leis from native flowers, learn to hula dance, create Hawaiian petroglyphs on tapa cloth, play ancient Hawaiian games, and even do some *Gyotaku* fish printing.

"The kids have such a good time they don't want to leave," he beams.

Victor gets it. He doesn't look at what he does as "just a job." He believes his work is important. He figures out how and where to add value. And Victor does one other thing: He assaults assumptions.

INNOVATION BEGINS WHERE ASSUMPTIONS END

The Irish playwright George Bernard Shaw explained the assumption-assaulting mindset well when he said: "The reasonable man adapts himself to the conditions that surround

him. The unreasonable man adapts surrounding conditions
to himself. Therefore, all progress depends on the unreasonable man."

Assumptions come in all shapes and sizes. They
include everything from our individual self-limiting beliefs,
conventional wisdom, what everybody "knows" to be
true, "the way we do things in this industry," conceptual
blocks, paradigms, and orthodoxies. It's only when we
challenge these assumptions that new, unbounded, unfet-
tered thinking can take place. Out of that process, original approaches can be spawned. Innovation begins where
assumptions end.

Spotting assumptions doesn't mean becoming a jerk,
however. You couldn't get through the day without making hundreds of assumptions, the vast majority of which are
completely accurate.

But it does mean that you need to get serious about thinking so that you can be your own best diagnostician when it
comes to identifying assumptions and determining whether
they are still valid.

Why is this important? Because time and again, social
scientific studies confirm that we humans tend to be a con-
forming-prone species.

"When people are faced with a majority of others who
agree on a particular attitude or judgment, they are very
likely to adopt the majority judgment," says Charlan Nemeth,
professor of psychology at the University of California,
Berkeley. "Even when using objective issues, such as judging
the length of lines, people will ignore the information from
their own senses and adopt an erroneous majority view."

The available evidence suggests two primary reasons why people tend to adopt the majority view, Charlan explains. "One is that people assume truth lies in numbers and are quick to infer that they themselves are incorrect when faced with a unanimous majority. The other reason is that they fear disapproval and rejection for being different."

In looking at assaulting assumptions—a vital I-Skill—I'll focus on three distinct types of assumptions: personal, organizational, and industry.

I. PERSONAL ASSUMPTIONS

The economist John Kenneth Galbraith once remarked, "Faced with having to change our minds or amassing the evidence to prove that we are right, we get busy on the proof."

What are your assumptions? What would you say is holding you back from achieving your goals, from reaching the next level of success?

Are there certain beliefs that come up over and over in your life? Here are a few possibilities to get you thinking:

- I don't have what it takes.
- Doing things with a lot of ambiguity scares me.
- I don't have the education.
- I'm not as smart as other people around here.
- I don't have the clout to get that promotion.
- I don't have the talent.
- I'm too old/too young.
- I don't have the self-discipline.
- I can't take responsibility.
- I'm trapped in my present job.

- I can't sell myself or my ideas effectively.
- I lack the energy.
- I'm not a self-starter.

If any of these defeatist mode statements resonate with you, it's important to realize that they are interpretations of reality and not necessarily facts. Unless you debunk them, they'll remain there to impede your progress.

Let's discuss two common personal assumptions in the following sections.

1. The "Title is All That Matters" Assumption

All too often the assumption is that the only power that matters is one's title. It's like the circus elephant that, while still young, is secured to a stake by a large chain attached to its leg. The baby elephant tries to break free but doesn't have the strength. Later, in adulthood, the elephant never attempts to break free again, although it would be easy to do so.

It's effortless to be cautious, subdued, and self-editing. It's reassuring to listen to the voice in your head when it says, "Better go easy on that; the boss might not like it. Play it safe; it's a tough job market out there."

In contrast, innovation-adept leaders cultivate the culture, even if it's not part of their job description.

You form the culture. All that is necessary for a terrible culture to triumph is for good people to do nothing to improve it day to day.

You can change the culture through simple acts. Rather than hoping somebody else will, speak up in town hall meetings. Ask questions of leadership. Contribute ideas to your firm's idea management process. Go the extra mile to help a colleague on a tight deadline. All of these are ways of improving your culture.

You don't need a title to make a difference.

2. The "Never Disagree with Your Boss" Assumption

If you have a useful contribution or an alternative suggestion that has potential merit, don't hide your light under a bushel. Smash the assumption that you can't disagree without being disagreeable.

"If I personally disagree with the leadership team," one manager told me, "I find ways to communicate that without damaging the relationships I've established."

That's exactly what Prakash I. did when legislation that would alter the rules of his industry was proposed by Congress. At first blush, the regulatory change appeared to spell the imminent disruption of the government stu-dent loan–servicing business and Prakash's company in particular.

The company's senior leadership team was quick to oppose the administration's proposal that the government take over the student loan industry. They assumed that fight-ing the proposed change was their primary option, and they began an effort to lobby Congress.

But as Prakash studied the issue, he began to see that without the cooperation of other industry competitors, con-fronting the proposed change would have little chance of success. Prakash could have easily told his boss what he knew the boss wanted to hear. Instead, he challenged the

70

"never disagree with your boss" assumption. Then he went to his manager with a fresh perspective on the issue.

"I started by defusing the personal aspect and establishing a common objective," Prakash recalled. "I asked my boss, 'What's our end goal? Do we want the U.S. to have choices in lending? Isn't our end goal to provide financial services?'"

Once they agreed on their goal, Prakash was able to express his disagreement by focusing on what was best for the company.

"From a lobbying standpoint, we spend very little compared to our competitors," Prakash told his boss. "And without a united front, our money doesn't go far. So the sooner we can find a way to service our customers in a way that aligns with the new policy, the sooner we can carve out a niche and get back to our mission. With this regulatory change, our primary customer will be the government instead of the banks. And although our margins will be lower, our volume will be much higher, meaning higher ultimate net income."

By challenging the assumption that employees should never disagree with their superiors, Prakash was able to successfully communicate his views to his boss and to the senior team. Prakash was proved right. The firm's shares soared when the company was awarded a contract to service a portion of the Department of Education's $550 billion in federal student loans. And Prakash was awarded a "seat at the table" in strategic decisions in the company and played an important role in the company's transition to a new business model.

"My job is a nice mix of the technical and business side," he told me. "It's very dynamic and always changing. I have a lot of autonomy, and I get to interact with some really great people. We have a lot of fun."

All because he was willing to challenge the prevailing assumption.

II. ORGANIZATIONAL ASSUMPTIONS

Just as personal assumptions can cloud individual thinking, certain biases and processes and ways of doing things become deeply ingrained in organizations. Let's discuss three common organizational assumptions.

1. The "We Don't Have Time to Innovate" Assumption

According to Harvard researcher Juliet Shorr, if you're employed, you're putting in 163 hours more each year (an extra month) than a similar person in the workforce 30 years ago. Clearly, "doing more with less" often means "doing more with fewer people." You and I are besieged with day-to-day, minute-to-minute demands and pressures like never before:

- The typical manager in a large organization now receives in excess of 150 e-mails a day, according to Gallup.
- According to the American Management Association, employees spend almost two hours reading and responding to these messages.
- Knowledge workers get interrupted, on average, every three minutes, according to research by the University of California, Irvine.

- Nielsen reports that, as of 2008, people sent and received an average of 7 phone calls and 12 text messages each day.
- Fully 25 percent of employees at large companies say their communications—voice mail, e-mail, and meetings—are nearly or completely unmanageable, according to a McKinsey survey of more than 7,800 workers around the world.

The result of all these intrusions? Employees are overconnected, overcommitted, overworked, and overwhelmed. One in three report their communications are "out of control."

Is it any wonder that one of the most common barriers to innovation that my client surveys reveal is "lack of time to innovate"? It inhibits creativity by crowding out reflection time that can produce fresh approaches. If you can't find time, how can you gather information about an idea, or catch up on your reading, or dream up your next breakthrough?

Nevertheless, "lack of time to innovate" is an assumption. The question at the heart of this assumption is this: If you and you colleagues had more time, would you produce more innovation? Would there be a greater tendency to discover and implement better processes, products, and services? Would hiring more people and cutting people's workload lead to more innovation? Or would the tendency be to simply expand the remaining workload to fill the available time?

Here's what I discovered: An abundance of time does not guarantee more creative output any more than a lack of time always means less innovation.

Innovators often point to a time crunch to meet a deadline that led them to stop ignoring a problem and come up with a novel solution. During such times, the inadequacies of present processes, methods, and procedures become obvious. In crunch times, the sales rep in the field office, when trying to process a rush order, has a "there's got to be a better way" moment and comes up with an idea to find that better method. The team preparing in haste for the industry trade show comes up with ideas that dramatically improve next year's planning. The marketing team, busy preparing a bid proposal by the promised deadline, is spurred to rethink its system so that next time doesn't require an all-nighter.

All of these are examples of how assaulting assumptions can turn the "lack of time" from a barrier to a catalyst. Necessity is the mother of innovation. Capacity is a state of mind. And innovation begins where assumptions end.

When "lack of time" surfaces in conversations or company surveys, delve deeper into the issue. Are people trying to send a message to senior management? Is there a more fundamental problem? Is lack of time symptomatic of a production-oriented culture that is uncomfortable with the whole idea of innovation and the need to take time to think?

2. The "You're Either Creative or You're Not" Assumption
Overturning this assumption is what this book is all about, so let's give it the attention it deserves.

David Campbell, Ph.D., a fellow at the Center for Creative Leadership in Greensboro, North Carolina, has studied creativity his entire professional career. "The people who don't believe they've been blessed with creativity think that it comes far more easily to creative people than it actually does," Campbell told me. "But if you ask people who use their creativity what the most popular misconception is, they tell you it's that other people think it is easy for them to be creative. The fact is it's not easy. It's really just a lot of hard work. You've got to try and fail, try and fail, and try and fail again."

Lee Clow is president and creative director of Chiat/Day Advertising. The firm's distinctive commercials for Apple, Nike, and many other clients have garnered a bevy of industry awards. But even for someone who has achieved such recognition, coming up with the next campaign is never easy.

"Mostly, you go down paths that lead nowhere," Clow said. "Sometimes you'll sit in front of a tablet or with three other people in a brainstorming session, and you'll just stare at each other. Absolutely nothing happens. The harder you try to make it come out of your brain, the more suppressed it gets. Then, all of a sudden, bam! What if we did it this way? Or: How about that way? Many times I've gotten up at 'O dark 30' and gone down to the kitchen and done the storyboard."

Certainly everyone isn't born with equal talents or abilities. Not everyone is capable of learning to paint like Picasso. But anyone can learn to be more creative in the workplace through the way he or she works with ideas. Business creativity, in other words, can be learned—and it's really not so complicated.

If you're attempting to innovate, you'll bump up against this still-prevailing misconception. Many, if not most, business leaders believe innovation is a rare gift that only a few people have, and these folks are, of course, at the top of the organization. Where else would they be? So while things are changing because of the "disrupt or be disrupted" imperative, the folks you work with may not have gotten the memo.

I don't mean to be dismissive, but this is what I've found in working with so many people over the years. This is one assumption you'll have to help your organization overcome. Be aware that doing this isn't a one-shot deal, and it won't happen overnight.

3. The "We Don't Have an Innovation Process" Assumption

Nancy Snyder is Whirlpool's innovation champion and architect of one of the world's most successful innovation processes. She wrote up the Whirlpool story in *Unleashing Innovation: How Whirlpool Transformed an Industry*. I asked her what she thought of the assumption that without an overarching innovation process in place, the individual at the bottom, or even the middle, of an organization has little chance of effecting change.

"That would be my premise," Nancy said, "that you can be really innovative but if the organization you work for doesn't change significantly, you're never going to get a chance to use your I-Skills.

"But let me go to your side because that's the side I'd rather be on," she continued. "I think of my MBA students getting ready to graduate into today's job market. They're realizing that if they put their learning on their resumes, all the tools they've learned for changing an organization's systems to embed innovation, that they've got an advantage [over

76

other applicants]. So I would agree with your premise: there's a lot you can do as an individual. And if your organization can't deal with it, go to a not-for-profit, do something in your life because innovation skills are so ubiquitous that you want to get practice at [using] them."

4. The "If You Fail, You're Fired" Assumption

When "Vince" heard that company leaders had mentioned the possibility of a new business venture regarding money management classes for students, he didn't think the idea would stay around for very long. But he went home, did some research, and realized that the idea was more viable than he thought. Excited by his findings, he spent the next two weeks developing a proposal that he plopped down on the table at the next meeting, much to the surprise of his co-workers and superiors.

After a few weeks of exchanging ideas and questions, senior management decided to support Vince's championing of the new business initiative, indeed to put him in charge. But there was a caveat attached. If Vince were to accept the position and fail, he would not be guaranteed another position.

Vince weighed his options carefully with his wife and decided to embrace the opportunity. He spent the next few months operating as a one-man business, taking care of sales, marketing, and operations. Things went well for a while, but six months in, he'd hit a wall. The chief operations officer left the company, and his industry began to undergo a major disruption. He had the option to finish what he had started in the attempt to secure his job, but

Vince knew that under the radically changing circumstances, it was not in the company's best interest to pursue his startup any longer.

"I went to [senior management] and told them that we needed to stop, and here's why. Sure, I was scared of being out of a job, and I didn't want to fail, but I saw beyond the possibility of getting fired and instead used the opportunity to communicate why I would continue to add value to the company if I was allowed to stay around."

Vince didn't just get to keep working there. He was promoted to Director of Business Development. It was his I-Skills that were needed in a time of crisis.

When I spoke with Tom Dolan, the Xerox sales innovator who proposed the idea that the company should move into services, he cut right to the heart of the "if you fail, you're fired" assumption. The real risk in possibly failing or falling short isn't so much with senior management. It's with your fellow managers and employees.

"In most cases that's not going to cost you your job," said Tom. "But you may have issues with your peer group. They may criticize your project's lack of results as their way of being heard. You're apt to hear about the negatives from a third party. . . . Some people [said our idea] was a pipe dream; it wasn't to my face, always to a third party. People would tell me, 'So and so thought you were out of your mind.'

"If you're going to innovate and receive the rewards of risk taking, you can't be worried what's going on in the background," said Dolan. "It's hard to get everybody on board. It's just the way corporations are and you have to deal with it. Those guys [who were skeptical of his idea] weren't out there talking to customers, so they didn't perceive the threat we faced. I clearly knew that challenging the assumption that we should move from being purely product driven to being service driven was not an easy task. But we prevailed and the results of this new strategy speak for themselves."

III. INDUSTRY ASSUMPTIONS

Just as individuals harbor assumptions, and organizations have them too, sometimes whole industries come under the grip of widely held, limiting beliefs.

A number of years ago I was invited by a trade association in the United States to conduct a workshop for their annual convention in Savannah. The meeting planner had been asked to book me by the program chair, who had heard me speak at another conference. The planner had very little involvement with the decision, and it showed in our introductory conversation.

"Well, okay," she sighed at one point, "I guess the guys will go for this topic. But around here we often say that a spring is a spring is a spring."

She meant that innovation and springs—the product category at the center of this association's reason for being—were about as far apart as the North and the South Poles. Springs are commodities. The spring buyers—the Big Three American auto companies and other large industrial companies—were interested in only getting the lowest possible price.

As I would learn, the industry was facing upheaval, and this was years before the bankruptcy and rebirth of General

Motors and Chrysler. Association conventions attracted the owners and general managers of spring manufacturers who were doing around $20 million in annual sales. They had become, in the words of one member, "pity parties." The automakers were beating them up for cost concessions, and many were facing declining margins, stiffer competition, and disappearing customers as industrial companies in America moved operations offshore.

As the engagement date loomed on my calendar, I became transfixed by that comment: "a spring is a spring is a spring."

If true, it challenged an assumption I'd held for years that there's no such thing as a truly mature market or a true commodity product. "There's only a tired imagination," I'd often say on the speaking platform. That may be great rhetoric, but what about the reality for members of this association. Maybe springs were true commodities after all.

I called the meeting planner and asked her for the names of 5 to 10 of the association's most successful company presidents.

As I interviewed these leaders, I found they opened up when I promised that our conversation was "off the record" and that I wouldn't relay their comments to the audience in Savannah. I asked each of them the same two questions: Is a spring just a commodity? Does anything differentiate your products except offering a lower price?

What I found in talking with these top company presidents confirmed my bias. A few were seeking new niche markets where they could offer differentiated product at higher margins, in effect firing their auto company customers altogether. Some were beginning to manufacturer more than just the spring; they were building entire components that surrounded their basic spring. Others were discovering new uses for springs on behalf of customer groups that, in the past, had used fasteners.

One president said to me, "A spring is nowhere near to being a commodity, because if it's not perfect for that [perceived] application, it doesn't work. In this industry, we've allowed our customers to convince us that a spring is a spring is a spring."

Here are four strategies for improving the quality of your thinking:

1. **Question the value of experience.**
2. **Look for your opening.**
3. **Cultivate a questioning mindset.**
4. **Take time to think about how you think.**

1. Question the Value of Experience

In his book *Outliers*, Malcolm Gladwell argues that 10,000 hours of experience is necessary to achieve mastery of any talent or field. With those numbers under your belt, you've built up a lot of answers. You're one big walking, talking "mechanical rule for solving a problem or dealing with a situation."

But experience can also infect us with biases that blind us to new possibilities. Past experience can prevent us from seeing how the world has changed and that a new generation of up-and-comers doesn't adhere to the same preconceived notions. They are willing to question the status quo.

Sometimes it's hard to sit in a meeting with some of these new ideas being bandied about when you remember the time "we tried that and it didn't work." And you're up to your ears in alligators, and "here we go again" on some wingding approach that somebody gets all jazzed up about because he or she wasn't there! Why reinvent the wheel? Why go down that path again just because some "facilitator" from the training department has asked everyone to keep an open mind. Give me a break.

Such situations call for a mental and emotional reset, which is not easy. My advice: Let the conversation play out and try to keep an open mind. The fact is, maybe the timing was off the last time or the execution was flawed.

Whatever the reason may have been, keep your mind open and question your experience.

2. Look for Your Opening

John G. is a sales strategy manager for a Hollywood studio. Over the years since he interned in my office while a student at the University of California, Santa Barbara, I've kept in touch with him and observed his career progress with great interest. The last time we met, when I asked him how things were going, he looked glum.

"It's a very high-pressure, time-sensitive position," he explained. "I have to get my stable of retail customers to decide on their order for a new DVD before the deadline my company has set so that we have sufficient time to get it made and shipped to them in time for its release."

Other departments (internal customers) are waiting for him to get the DVD made for that movie. Competition with other studios for shelf space is fierce. And the media industry, caught up in its own disruptions, keeps the pressure at the boiling point.

When I asked John about the culture where he works, he revealed the source of his discouragement. "I see too many examples of promotions based on connections and favoritism," he said. "Like the woman who had a child with one of the senior executives. She got accepted into a special course for high-potential managers."

One co-worker actually came up with a wonderful idea for a top retail customer: Have an Asian section of movie titles in the home entertainment section if the retailer was in a predominantly Asian market and to do the same for other demographic markets. The retailer loved the idea and adopted it.

"But she didn't receive the credit she should have," John says. "She was only recognized within our group of 30, not companywide, and did not receive a promotion."

In his own job, he believes he has been thwarted at every turn.

"I undertook a huge project in which I wrote up a white paper with a proposal about how to raise public awareness of a new product, and how to increase sales. I contacted our research department and received stacks of papers that I used in my proposal. I built an argument about increasing new product sales by promoting it as PlayStation 3-compatible. But once I submitted it to the VP of my department, I never heard anything back.

"I didn't give up; I attached it again in a later e-mail, reminding him about it. But to this day, I've never heard anything back. No 'thanks for your input,' or 'great ideas, good job,' nothing. I put weeks of time and effort into it and heard nothing. And I'm even lucky enough to have some great contacts within the company."

Caught up in the daily grind, it is easy to lose your sense of possibility and give in to prevailing assumptions. John sees his workplace culture as political and unfair, and he assumes merit will not be eventually rewarded. He tried to show initiative only to be shut down. It would be easy for him to give in to his sustainer mode of thinking, to mentally check out and become cynical, and find interests outside of work to engage him.

When I asked John what else he was doing to differentiate himself, a glimmer brightened his eyes. "A lot of people here don't even know the financial terms we use, so I'm one of three MBAs who have been asked to teach a class for co-workers to help them understand the financial side better."

Suddenly it hit me. "That's it," I blurted out. "That class is your unique opportunity to break out of the pack. That class is your opportunity to use what you know that other people don't have! When you teach a class, you have the rare chance to share not just your knowledge but also your point of view. People who attend your class will come to know you as a person. How might you use these classes to build your internal reputation as both a team player and as a master of the business side? You've got to create the most user-friendly, fun, interactive course imaginable."

For John, assaulting assumptions means that he doesn't grow cynical in a tricky situation. He needs to continue to hone and use his I-Skills, even if there is no reward bestowed by his bosses. He must continue to look for opportunities to differentiate himself and add unique value, while adhering to his personal innovation strategy.

3. Cultivate a Questioning Mindset

Michael Ray was a marketing professor at Stanford University when he saw the need to address a gap in the curriculum. Although students were learning a great deal about the algorithmic side of business, they were learning next to nothing about the heuristic side.

Michael organized a class for undergraduates called Personal Creativity in Business. He taught business students to meditate and to suspend judgment. He taught that innovation is a way of life. "The creativity I'm talking about is different from problem solving," he explained. "It's different from just coming up with ideas. People have enough ideas. The real question is, 'Which ideas are you going to use?'"

In short order it became the class hardest to get into. For years, he'd invite some of the most ingenious entrepreneurs from nearby Silicon Valley to come speak to his students.

Distilling the collective wisdom of everything he'd learned into his classic 1986 book *Creativity in Business*, Ray suggested wacky little reminders like "Ask dumb questions."

"If you're willing to ask a dumb question," he wrote, "you just may get a smart answer."

When it comes to assumption assaulting, questions are where it's at. Journalists are taught to answer the who/what/where/when/why of any story, lest they confound the reader. The Japanese have given the world their "five why" question. Its name stems from the Japanese management belief that asking "why" at least five times gets to the root cause of a problem.

Whatever you see, ask yourself why it is the way it is. If you don't get an answer that makes sense, perhaps there is room for further pondering and changing for the better. Why is our production line set up this way? Why do we track that metric? Who knows a better way to handle that?

Becoming an assumption assaulter starts with cultivating a questioning mindset. Questions help you heal from the disease called "hardening of the attitudes." It breaks up the compacted "soil" inside our brains, so that, with cultivation and care, a thousand ideas can bloom. Questions help you reframe the issue so you can think bigger about the possibilities. Questions also help you redefine the nature of the problem. Sometimes they can help you discover the right question to ask.

At one manufacturing plant, shop floor workers were asked for suggestions on how to improve productivity. None were given. A short time later, a similar group of workers was asked this question: "How can we make your job easier?" A torrent of ideas came pouring out.

So ask your questions and then ask more. Peel away the layers of assumptions to get at the heart of the issue. It's not a new tool; it's been around at least since Socrates. But it still works.

4. Take Time to Think about How You Think
The dizzying pace of business and of organizational life today means that there will always be a reason for avoiding fundamental thinking. Henry Ford said, "Thinking is the

86

hardest work there is, which is probably the reason why so few engage in it."

You delay thinking about issue X while you attend to the everyday activity, which never ends. So you pass the buck. You delegate thinking about issue X to someone else on the team, outsource it to a supplier, or pass it to a subordinate for "further research." You delay right up to deadline and then default to option A, or "whatever the consensus is at the meeting."

You rationalize and make excuses, such as:

- Those who demonstrate independent thinking are usually perceived as threats.
- They don't pay me to think; they pay me to execute.
- I'm a specialist; I'm really not trained to look at the big picture.
- Taking risks and questioning the status quo are not rewarded in my company and often are punished.
- The people who rise to the top are not assumption assaulters; they're efficient at implementing ideas from other people.
- Around here, short-term performance is what gets rewarded.
- People who engage in independent thinking are often perceived as threats where I work.

Making yourself indispensable at work means not buying these assumptions. Rather, thinking original thoughts, expanding your own point of view, and identifying a fatal flaw without casting blame are marks of an innovation-adept leader.

In an economy of disruption, downsizing, and discontinuity, we're all involved in more and more complex decisions, and we have less and less time to reflect on the options and implications. Reminding ourselves to look for the unidentified assumptions in the issue at hand may prove to be the best tool of all.

HOW TO MASTER THIS I-SKILL

Your reputation, perhaps more than you realize, rests on your original, nonherd thinking. Using this I-Skill means bringing a fresh perspective to bear as often as possible, and in a constructive, rather than critical, judgmental, and negative manner.

Mastering the I-Skill of assaulting your assumptions requires that you practice this skill every day, with a foremost emphasis on becoming aware of personal assumptions. It's time to hone these skills into a competitive differentiator for yourself and your firm.

Here are my suggestions for taking action:

1. Remember that innovation often begins where assumptions end. So talk back to the voices in your head that emerge out of defeatist, sustainer, and dreamer modes of thinking. Cultivate a questioning mindset. Remember that asking questions is the most powerful spur to jumpstart new thinking.
2. If you don't like the choices on the table, ask yourself (and others) what a third or fourth choice might look like. If you're facing unpromising or onerous choices in

a team or work group, take initiative. Be the one who suggests, "Hey, everybody, it looks like maybe we've prematurely limited ourselves to options A and B. Why don't we all try to come up with C and D just for the heck of it?" Do this with a smile in your voice, just so people don't think you're being a troublemaker.

As you begin to use this skill on a daily basis, you'll find it broadens your horizons and boosts your percceived value even if people can't quite identify why. This I-Skill is particularly valuable when your organization faces big changes. And that's the subject of the next chapter.

I-Skill # 3

Cultivate a Passion for the End Customer

Everything You Create Is Your Product and Every Product Has a Customer

I ran into Steve Jobs at Dulles Airport in Washington. "You're Steve Jobs," I said, reaching out my hand with a big smile.

He ignored my hand. "Who are you?" he said.

Steve is not the glad-handing type. It was awkward, and I wished I hadn't done it. I guess I couldn't help myself because I'm one of his biggest fans.

From an early age, Steve Jobs has been in the spotlight. Since he appeared on the cover of *Time* at 26, everybody wants a piece of him. Everyone wants to say they know him and tell their friends about him.

I follow his career. I think about him every time I use my iPhone or listen to my iPod while running or working out at the gym. I feel connected to the man who wouldn't shake my hand because he was my advocate in coming up with some "insanely great products" in his time.

Steve was able, through his personality, charisma, vision, and smarts, to demand the best from a team. Then he propelled them to go beyond what they thought was best and onto a breakthrough. Millions of other end users and I are the beneficiaries.

Earlier this year, in Orlando, I asked 100 or so senior product developers from companies like Caterpillar, Hewlett Packard, and John Deere what product they'd adopted that "rocked their world." Someone blurted out "iPhone," and there were murmurs of agreement. But then the room was quiet. Apparently it is easier to talk about innovation than to produce it.

Steve Jobs produces products that rock people's worlds. How? By getting vast teams of specialists to collaborate and to understand that second-best efforts will be unacceptable. That includes the guys who know batteries and the people who are world-class with plastics, because Steve's got to have the perfect plastic for the face of that phone and he's not going to settle for anything less. He will not sell an inferior product to his customers.

You may not think that you create products for a living, and you are probably quite convinced that mimicking Steve's style will not get you anywhere but out the door. Being controlling and seeking perfection? Out! Demanding quality and excellence? To a point maybe, but better not ruffle feathers.

After all, isn't it best to go along to get along? Compromise? Give in? Don't make enemies?

Here's the reality. You do create products for a living. That slide deck you're working on for the meeting in Chicago—that's a product. The new cost-reduction initiative you're contributing to is a product. Even that e-mail memo you sent out five minutes ago is a product.

Everything you create is your product—and every product has a customer.

So how do you differentiate and become indispensable where you work? You invent a steady stream of insanely great "products" that better serve the needs of your end customer, whether internal (employees in other departments in your organization who depend on you to get their work done) or external (those who buy your firm's products and services in the marketplace).

To illustrate this point, let's pay a visit to two contributors who have this passion for the customer in spades.

WATCH JENNIFER ROCK HER WORLD

Several years ago, *The Wall Street Journal* reported an unusual cost-cutting method adopted by the national electronics retailer Circuit City. The Virginia-based company announced that it had fired all its top salespersons. They did so not because these employees were doing a bad job or because the company was downsizing.

They did it because the employees cost too much money. They were being replaced with new hires who agreed to work for a lower wage and no benefits.

I read that little squib with my morning coffee and just sort of scratched my head. Commentators chided the company for callousness. Even to the coldest-hearted capitalist, it just didn't sit right. What kind of data encouraged such a decision?

Circuit City's bone-headed move turned out to be the beginning of a death march. The chain declared bankruptcy several years later.

In Minnesota, another electronics retailer chose a much smarter strategy to deal with the tough economy. There was a different philosophy at Best Buy: "Treat our employees well, and they'll take good care of the customers."

Electronics retailing is not for the faint of heart. And even though Best Buy became the only national electronics retailer still standing in the United States when Circuit City went out of business, it won't necessarily be easier for the company because of new competition from Wal-Mart, Costco, and others who are expanding into their turf.

To compete, Best Buy initiated an improved-value proposition. They oriented the company around the needs and behaviors of its core customers. Then Best Buy's communications team adopted the principles of this strategy and applied them to the unmet needs of employees and business partners.

Jennifer Rock is Director of Dialogue and Intranet, an eight-person team within Best Buy's Department of Employee Communications, a position she created from scratch. Why would a company give a darn about listening to its employees? Why would they add to their headcount in challenging times?

"Our success, as with any retailer, boils down to the interaction between one customer and one employee,"

Jennifer explains. "Is that employee happy and productive and informed and excited? I need to know that employee's state of mind better than anyone else in the company. [The department has] to have a passion for our employees because that's who we serve."

With this rationale, Jennifer convinced Best Buy's senior management that the new dialogue team wouldn't cost—it would pay!

"We are not a profit center that brings in sales for the company," Jennifer explained. "But happy, productive, informed employees tend to stay with the company longer than those who aren't. Best Buy's U.S. employee turnover two years into the program was still at 81 percent, but in the next three years had dropped to 60 percent. A year later, turnover was at an all-time best of 49 percent. Larger studies have shown that staying with a company and feeling engaged is due, in large part, to how the communication is flowing: how your manager is communicating with you, how your peers and interpersonal communication affect you."

Best Buy has thousands of stores under multiple brands in the United States and other countries. Jennifer's team's mission is to connect all 160,000 employees with information and to provide multiple channels for employees to be heard on any number of issues regarding their working lives.

To accomplish this, the communications team conducts weekly polls; organizes the Water Cooler (the official company online discussion forum); sponsors agenda-free town hall meetings with senior managers, both live and via virtual chat space; and provides a special one-on-one connection called The Chair.

Establishing the new department was anything but easy. Jennifer's team faced a scant budget for data gathering and inexperience with audience research techniques.

I asked her how they could keep costs so low.

"We try things that are low cost and minimally disruptive," she told me. "The Chair came from my colleague, Jill, who was watching TV one night. A Kleenex commercial came on, where they had a sofa for people to share how they were feeling. She came in the next day and said, 'I want to sit in a chair in a busy area in the building.' Jill has an empty chair next to her, and employees just sit down and talk to her. They know she will listen and then do something with that information."

Jennifer and her team were able to prove their passion for their customers (the employees) when company leaders decided to reduce the employee discount.

"The move set off a firestorm with employees," she remembers. "On the Water Cooler [online forum], hundreds and hundreds of employees talked about what this discount meant to them, and what it meant to customers, since employees could try out products and recommend them to customers. People wrote in to suggest other ways the company could save money without touching the employee discount. The company leaders changed their mind."

Jennifer's team, and the company leaders, recognized that this was how they needed to run the company. "[Senior management] said to us, 'The next time you see something like this and we are unaware of a groundswell happening, you have permission to kick down the door. Don't even knock. We need to know.' And that's when I thought, 'Wow, we are adding value.'"

Jennifer Rock personifies the I-Skill of passion for the customer, in her case the internal customer. She noticed how the marketing tools Best Buy used to understand its end customers could be applied to understanding its 160,000 employees, and she took action.

FIVE WAYS TO FOCUS ON YOUR INTERNAL AND EXTERNAL CUSTOMERS

Since everything we create is our product, and every product has a customer, the best products are those that anticipate the customer's need and offer a superior solution. What follows are five methods designed to help you create "insanely great products."

---

1. **Understand the business you're in.**

2. **Develop empathy for the customer.**

3. **Strive for a big picture perspective.**

4. **Take on the customer's problem.**

5. **Treat your boss like a customer**

Let's take a look.

1. Understand the Business You're In

What are people buying from you?

My friend, Dr. Michael LeBoeuf, author of *The Greatest Management Principle in the World*, observes that the only two things people buy are solutions to their problems and good feelings. If that's true, what business are you in?

Revlon founder Charles Revson was asked at a party, "What do you sell?" The cosmetic king answered, "I sell hope."

Ted Levitt, the great marketing professor at Harvard University, used to say that people didn't buy drills. They bought a device that would carve out a quarter-inch hole in their wall so that they could hang a picture.

Revson was on to the "good feelings" and Levitt was on to the "solutions to their problems" aspects of being customer-focused.

Whether you're an individual contributor, a supervisor, or a departmental manager, it helps to know the business you are really in. If you're in sales, you're in the business of providing solutions to customer problems. If you lead the benefits section of your company's human resources department, you are also in the solutions business, although your customers are internal rather than external. Beyond this, though, are those few who understand that producing good feelings is the little bit extra that raises their stature in the organization.

2. Develop Empathy for the Customer

Empathy is the ability to walk in another person's shoes and experience things through his or her eyes. It's different from sympathy, which is feeling sorry for another person.

Kevin and Jackie Freiberg, authors of the book *Nuts*, describe how enthusiasm for raising on-time performance for Southwest Airlines' external customers (passengers) led one employee to do the unexpected. The station manager in the Los Angeles airport (LAX)—where a lot of originating flights leave every day—put a team together to go visit down-line airports in Albuquerque, Phoenix, San Jose, and Sacramento that receive those originating flights.

They asked the down-line station teams the same question: "What are the top 10 things we do in Los Angeles that make your jobs more difficult?" The team would then bring that feedback back to LAX, identify the irritants, and get right to work making improvements.

Notice the I-Skills being used here: The LAX station manager took initiative. Rather than do a perfunctory phone survey to get this "got to do" off her list, she put a team together and went to visit internal customers in person. By creating a listening environment, she displayed empathy for employees and external customers alike.

The vast majority of people who work in organizations have absolutely no contact with customers, so they don't have an obvious reason to develop empathy. (Those in sales, customer service, and so on, are the exception.)

So when I talk about empathy for the customer, I'm really talking about understanding the internal customers you and your department serve. That means your boss, as well as the folks whom you and your department or division serves. They, in turn, produce the goods and services that will be delivered to the end customers.

Most principles of serving end customers apply to three types of needs: present needs, unmet needs, and unarticulated needs.

The present needs of customers are well known. These are the projects you're working hard on right now to deliver on time. But if you're trying to make innovation your business, and make a significant impact, you also have to consider the unmet needs (customers want what you produce better/cheaper/faster) and the unarticulated needs (those that customers don't consciously realize they "need" until they've experienced the value of your new way of solving their problem).

3. Strive for a Big Picture Perspective

One way to jump-start innovation toward unmet and unarticulated needs is to pause and think, with a strategy, about the big picture. Ask yourself where your organization needs to go and what it needs to do now. Is the company attempting to reduce costs, per the recent mandate from the chief executive officer (CEO)? Is it trying to leverage economies of scale, or to avoid having to lay people off? Is it trying to integrate numerous information technology (IT) systems after a recent acquisition or merger, or reinventing its business model because of a major disruption? Or going green?

By becoming aware of, and focusing on, an unmet need, you can begin imagining unconventional and untried ways you and your department can meet that goal. Every business has problems and unmet objectives. But not everybody thinks about these needs. Instead, they target only what's on their plate. In selling any idea to your boss, and your boss's boss, it's important to put these objectives front and center.

4. Take on the Customer's Problem

"We are training an entire generation of assistant marketing managers that, if they have five good bullet points on a slide, they think they understand the business," says Dev Patnaik, founder and chief executive of Jump Associates and the author of *Wired to Care: How Companies Prosper When They Create Widespread Empathy*. "They don't realize that their business is out in the world—in the stores where people are buying their products and services, and in the homes where they live their lives."

Your organization's challenge is to create new value for customers, and value is in the eyes and ears and taste buds of the beholder. Yet, because so many parties in the organization and in the larger "value chain" provide their contributions, it's easy to lose sight of this.

"We never look out the window," was a complaint I heard at a consumer reports–type organization. "We are so darn busy inside these four walls we become insular. 'That's the business side's responsibility' or 'It's not my job' is the usual attitude. Then a crisis hits, like a competitive upset that causes our products to fall out of favor with the marketplace, and all hell breaks loose."

Companies assume that because they have so many customers today, tomorrow will be the same. Sorry, but there is just no guarantee that they will stay with you.

Do you want to develop your passion for customers into a full-on I-Skill? It's not that difficult to expand into a unique point of view. Step outside the bubble of your culture, interact with enough people, and listen to what they say. This will give you a sense of what that outside world thinks, feels, and perceives about your company, as opposed to what people inside assume.

Strive to acquire empathy for the end customer, no matter who you perceive that customer to be. And keep this in mind: You do this even when those voices in your head keep going off about how senior management couldn't care less as long as everybody is meeting their numbers.

5. Treat Your Boss Like a Customer

On a recent flight, I chatted with Fred, a young supervisor who works for a multinational foods company on the West Coast. It didn't take long to figure out that Fred was frustrated in his career. He likes his work, gets on well with his key retail accounts, and enjoys managing the nine people who report to him. Nonetheless, he is experiencing trouble with his boss, who's two years younger than he is.

"He's always stealing my ideas," Fred confided. "I'm thinking of looking for another job." As we discuss his situation, there's no question Fred's boss feels threatened by his charge. Fred described being in a meeting with a cross-functional team, most of whom were more senior level, poring over a chart on one client's book of business. Suddenly Fred had a realization.

"We're looking at the problem all wrong," he exclaimed. "It's actually going to take us seven years to break even on this client." The numbers were quickly crunched and, sure enough, with Fred's new perspective used as the base of analysis, the higher-ups in the room "get this look on their faces that says, 'Bravo,'" Fred recalled with a mixture of pride and pain.

Fred's boss, also in the meeting, was anything but congratulatory. He felt one-upped, threatened. And on it goes, this tension between Fred and his boss. Fred leaned in to ask: "What should I do?"

"First off," I suggested, "be glad your manager is stealing your ideas. This is proof that you're coming up with ideas in the right vein. Isn't coming up with ideas really why you were hired? In addition to your regular work of managing key relationships, you are given specific issues like gathering data and crunching numbers and interpreting the outcome. Then you run everything through your imagination and produce value-adding ideas.

"Your boss is the buyer of your ideas," I continued, "just as you are the 'buyer' of ideas handed over to you by your reports. These ideas are like OEM parts that go into a manufactured product and don't all get 'Intel Inside' stickers giving credit. So, harsh as it might seem, get over it. But know this: Your time will come. If you have proven that you can produce ideas—the currency of the Innovation Age—the quality of your ideas will become evident without your needing to grandstand.

"On the other hand," I continued, "if your manager lacks ideas, demonstrates no imagination, doesn't understand how to add value for his up-line 'customers' (senior management), well, guess what, they'll discover this soon enough. If his success is solely dependent on poaching your ideas, he's toast—it's just a matter of time!"

Keep the ideas coming—they are the reason you have a job.

I-Skill #4

Think Ahead of the Curve

Notice Trends, Anticipate Threats, and Discover Hidden Opportunities

I take a flashlight with me on trips. I carry one in my car. We've got five flashlights around our house.

You're probably thinking, "What's the big deal? Why all the flashlights?"

I learned the value of a flashlight years ago, on a backpacking trip in the Grand Teton Mountains of Wyoming. The first day out, I stopped hiking toward evening, pitched my tent, and made supper. Then, with some daylight left, I decided to check out the neighborhood.

I meandered across a broad meadow full of scrub, scampered on a ways, and eyed a small oval-shaped lake. The setting sun broadcast the most amazing colors. I sat down on a log to take in the scene, and when I got up to go back to my tent, I noticed how dark it had gotten all of a sudden. As I started back to my tent, I worried about tripping over a rock or smacking into a tree. The next couple of hours I walked around with my hands out in front of me, trying to feel my way to my tent.

Giving up, I huddled underneath a pine tree with a Forest Service topographic map as my blanket. Since it was summer, I was in no danger of freezing to death. Still, it was a tad uncomfortable out there, especially when it started to rain.

When daylight appeared, I looked around. There was my tent—30 feet away!

Out of this experience, I learned two lessons.

First, being close to shelter does you zero good.

Second, things happen fast when you aren't paying attention.

Just as it does in businesses, organizations, and careers, a disruption can "suddenly" bombard you, too. Sales "all of a sudden" drop like the Teton sun. Out of the blue your department takes a hit, jobs are threatened, and everyone wonders what will happen and what to do.

In today's hypercompetitive world, you need your own version of a flashlight. With it in hand, you will find things do not happen quite so suddenly. You'll often find that the seeds of disruption were actually germinating for quite some time, if only we were tracking the trends with a willingness to assault our assumptions about what those trends signaled.

Although nobody can predict the future, mastering this chapter's I-Skill—thinking ahead of the curve—will give you a heads up on threats and opportunities in time to take responsive action.

Sure, some disruptions materialize so fast that almost nobody sees them coming or understands their severity. But by developing the ability to track emerging trends, and to assess and interpret the changes as they relate to your world, you are positioned to transform them into new opportunities and strategic advantage for yourself, your organization, and your career.

No matter the kind of work you do or the industry you're in, you can get better at anticipating what's ahead.

Everybody can get better at seeing problems and emerging opportunities and get ready with solutions. That's the focus of this chapter—to help you become indispensible to your organization by virtue of your skills in this area. Leaders who wait until all the data are clear usually wind up following the herd. And these days, following the herd does not differentiate you; it only makes you redundant. So let's pay a visit to an innovation-adept leader who used this I-Skill to rethink and redesign the entire back-office operations of a global company and fuel his career.

HOW PROCTER & GAMBLE'S CIO THINKS AHEAD

In Cincinnati I met Filippo Passerini, Procter & Gamble's hard-charging chief information officer (CIO). He is a fascinating guy—Ph.D. in statistics from the University of Rome, father of three, technical mountain climber. And he's the toast of his organization for what he and his troops have been able to accomplish for the good of the company.

Passerini was the driving force behind Procter's radical revamping of its back-office operations. The move obliterated $1.2 billion in costs from Procter & Gamble. It enabled the consumer products giant to respond quickly to the Global Economic Crisis and to bring new products to market faster than ever.

So how does Filippo unwind after routinely putting in 60-hour weeks? He plays chess. "Thinking what your opponent will do three moves out is good discipline for business," he told me in a thick Italian accent.

Filippo is the perfect illustration of the power of thinking ahead of the curve.

"It was our reading of trends that led us to make this move," he explained. In frequent open-ended brainstorming sessions, he and his core team of five saw that the world was shifting. It was moving from "big is good" to "flexible is good" to "network is good."

"Fifteen years ago, if you were a big company, that was a competitive advantage. Then flexibility was the way to achieve it. But we saw that over the next five years the network would become more and more important." What to do?

Passerini's vision was that the entire company should operate from one consolidated, integrated global network. He and his team assaulted the assumption that the way Procter & Gamble handled back-office functions like finance and accounting, human resources, facilities management, and information technology (IT) was good enough. They knew it was riddled with duplication

108

and waste. So they set forth to build a new unit—Global Business Services—to take over and consolidate all such operations.

Today, shared-services centers in Costa Rica; Manila, Philippines; and Newcastle, England, provide networked support around the clock to Procter & Gamble operations everywhere. All nonstrategic activities have been outsourced to outside vendors. And Passerini and his group have "de-commoditized ourselves" from being an internal service provider to becoming a strategic partner to the organization.

"One of our pillars is thinking out in the future and anticipating what is coming and then making your move. It's so much better than reacting."

Innovation-adept leaders like Filippo Passerini don't just gather better intelligence. They creatively crunch this data, argue about it, debate its implications, and try to connect the dots in some meaningful fashion. They seek to arrive at a point of view, both individually and collectively, about how to turn today's rapid changes into tomorrow's opportunities. And then they take action.

How are you "sussing out" the trends in your market and in your industry and in the wider world? What's new in your information diet that's stimulating your thinking? What trends, emerging technologies, and developments are you doing deep dives on to gain a knowledge edge?

"I manage my life like a chess game," Passerini told me as I was leaving. "I still continue to study every day."

Not bad advice for all of us.

EIGHT COMPONENTS TO THINKING AHEAD OF THE CURVE

If you want to be like Filippo Passerini and think ahead of the curve, there are eight rules to follow. They are:

1. **Audit your information diet.**
2. **Think of yourself as the eyes and ears of your organization.**
3. **Build your information and support networks.**
4. **Seek out forward-thinking, idea-oriented people.**
5. **Master the art of the deep dive.**
6. **Develop your point of view on key issues.**
7. **Connect the dots.**
8. **Give people permission to give you bad news.**

1. Audit Your Information Diet

In the early 1950s, victims of polio, most of them children, were dying at the rate of 58,000 per year in the United States alone, with more than 300,000 cases reported. Teams of scientists were working around the clock to develop a vaccine, but the solution was long in coming. Then an obscure University of Pittsburgh researcher named Jonas Salk broke through. His unconventional solution was to develop a killed virus vaccine. Everyone else had been working on the assumption that a live virus was the source of the solution.

Today there are almost no reported cases of polio.

I once had the privilege of interviewing Salk on a five-hour flight across the United States. I found him to be blunt and eager to debate and engage on the topic at hand (he'd just published a book called *World Population and Human Values*). After I referred several times to a book I'd been reading, Salk paused and asked, "Where is this book you refer to? Do you have a copy?" When I produced it from my bag, Salk speed-read it for 30 minutes before handing it back to me. He then ticked off an impressive compare and contrast to his own ideas on several points.

I was impressed. Jonas Salk had a take-charge attitude about information and new ideas, and it showed. Yet he wasn't unique in this respect.

In my 22-year study and observation of innovators in all fields of endeavor, I'm continually amazed at how "voracious appetite for new information" describes a characteristic they share. They work at keeping abreast with uncommon passion. They pore over data. They are eager and curious readers. They subscribe to, or monitor online, a variety of publications. They read the latest books.

Using every available opportunity for absorbing new information and ideas, they network all the time and seek out people who are knowledgeable in subjects they want to learn more about. They ask questions, probe deeply, and open their minds to what the answers mean. Wherever they are—at conferences, at social events, while passing through airports—they are alert for news they can use.

Innovators take this I-Skill seriously because it forms the basis of everything else they are and do. It's the nexus of their personal value proposition. Their superior intake informs their worldview and serves as an "early warning system" to alert them to the need to alter their point of view or direction. Also, it brings them superior ideas.

"I almost feel like a fake," one manager said. "People think I've come up with all these ideas, but in fact I've just gotten them from someplace else, usually from my reading."

Take a moment right now to ponder your "information diet" and what you've added of late. What stands out? That article you read this morning on the Internet? The conference call you participated in last evening on a special team you are involved with? The deck of slides from a fellow board member of your professional society? The conversation you had last week with a key member of your core network?

Then ask yourself: Is my information diet the best it can be, or do I need to make changes? Do I often discover trends when they are still in their infancy, or do I find that I constantly have to play catch up to what other people already seem to know about? Do I tend to surf the Internet aimlessly, or am I focused? How do I approach new topics? Do I tend to spend my reading time dwelling on the details of the latest scandal or disaster or taking the time to absorb articles whose content is well-researched, documented, and on a topic that I need to know more about?

Your diet is composed of information you consume by virtue of what you expose yourself to. How nutritious is your diet?

2. Think of Yourself as the Eyes and Ears of Your Organization

Innovation-adept leaders think of themselves as the organization. They regard themselves as its eyes, ears, and nose, even if that organization numbers in the hundreds of thousands.

They are listening nodes, marketplace sensing devices, discoverers of new best practices, hunters of future trends. They gather from the conferences they attend and the social networking contacts they nurture. They constantly refresh their mindset, upgrade and add to their skill set, and restock their tool sets for the days ahead.

Part of it is just a natural curiosity and love of learning. Another part is strategic: They know that the ability to hatch a compelling and value-adding idea depends on voluminous and timely inputs from the larger environment. They know that the raw materials entering their personal "idea factories" are bits of information, facts, and insight that can coalesce into new solutions, new customer benefits, new products or services, or cost-saving ideas.

When you think of yourself as the eyes and ears of your organization, people will notice. Colleagues will notice that you always seem to have better information at your disposal. They will pay attention when you share pertinent facts and contribute relevant examples. Senior managers will come to think of you as someone they can call on to contribute useful observations. They will begin to rely on you to keep them informed, up-to-date, knowledgeable, and focused on the big picture.

When you develop a reputation as someone interested in the future, you're more likely to be asked to help your organization create the future. You're more likely to be part of a cross-functional team or project tasked with finding new revenue streams, accomplishing a transformation of your company's culture, or creating a new business model.

Will you be ready? What value will you bring to the task?

My suggestion is this: Get ready in advance by thinking of yourself as the eyes and ears of your organization. What's going on out there that your organization or department needs to know about? Who's monitoring technological, demographic, social, and economic trends in your organization? How can you reach out to these people and demonstrate your interest?

Get serious about disseminating that information to people who need to know or would benefit from knowing. Sooner rather than later, you'll gain a perspective on what these "ahead of the curve" projects are going to be or should be. Then scope out which ones have the greatest potential of producing breakthroughs for your company and attach yourself to them.

Make competitive intelligence your competitive edge.

3. Build Your Information and Support Networks

Eleanor Roosevelt once said, "I made the discovery long ago that very few people made a great difference to me. But those few mattered enormously. I live surrounded by people, and my thoughts are always with the few that matter, whether they are near or far."

People also surround you. Perhaps, like the pioneering First Lady, you rely on a select few as well. These chosen few are your core network. "My network is where I get some of my best ideas," said John Draper, vice president of marketing at Mead Consumer Products. "I have a small number of people that I talk to fairly regularly, and we have a good exchange of ideas."

The members of your core network might be certain members of your family whose loyalty to you is deep, whose candor and supportiveness see you through good times and bad, sickness and health. They might be acquaintances you first met in college or in prior positions. What they have in common is not only the way you exchange information but also what they do to your thinking and the decisions you are wrestling with. They stimulate your forward thinking, and they encourage you to think big. There is no need not to be candid and confidential in the information you reveal. With your core network of supporters, trust is sacred.

Nurturing this network, even during 50-hour work-weeks, is essential. These people are closest to you in the sense that Eleanor Roosevelt described. They are less apt to "fall off your radar." But even this core group needs attention, giving, and sharing if you expect to call upon these folks for feedback, a shoulder to cry on, or someone to brag to when you've had a success episode.

There are two core networks.

1. Your internal/external network: Not only do people in this group watch your back, they also help you watch for the emerging trends and changes they are coping with. They share how they are making sense of and trying to capitalize on these developments.
2. Your expertise network: "I would recommend developing an expertise network," says Christopher Rollyson, the social networking maven. "It should include colleagues inside and outside your organization. People are not always able to take the time to attend meetings, so [join] the forums on social networking sites like

LinkedIn." Rollyson participates in 25 forums and says it doesn't take that much time.

Through other social networking sites like Facebook, MySpace, and your own network, you can reach hundreds and even thousands of others. But I'm with Eleanor Roosevelt in that we can have time, and heart space for, only a few if they are going to truly matter. Nurture them and be good to them, and they will see you through the disruptions and the tough times. Be there for them on their unexpected journeys, their strange decisions, and their passions that you do not share. If you've chosen well, they will be there for you. Give them wide berth, and they will give you wise counsel. Forgive them their nerdiness, and they shall forgive you. At all times, go with a spirit of loyalty and put others before yourself.

Asked how she handled networking, one manager said it was simple. "I just look at the names of people in my network, and ask myself, 'Who do I need to make contact with? How are they doing?' I reach out to them with a note or e-mail and just touch base and let them know I'm thinking of them."

She had it right.

In your people-saturated environment, you can get so busy going from one meeting or business trip to the next. It's too easy to get out of touch. Don't let it happen to you and your core network.

4. Seek Out Forward-Thinking, Idea-Oriented People
Take half an hour and go for a refreshing "walkie-talkie," where you converse while getting some fresh air and exercise.

It is amazing how many of the innovators we interviewed told us they got most of their ideas from being around other idea-oriented people. They get "fired up" during their conversations and often come away with dozens of new ideas. Idea people are friends, colleagues, co-workers, and neighbors who use ideas in their own lives. These are folks who get excited when you express your ideas and who enjoy talking about their own.

Take a moment right now and make a list of the people you know who stimulate your creativity when you are around them. Then ask yourself how you can arrange to spend more time with these people without slighting your other responsibilities. If there aren't such persons in your life right now, resolve to do something about it. For instance, you can attend meetings of organizations in your field or profession. Through conscious effort, you can and will increase the number of idea-oriented people you count as friends.

By nurturing and building your networks, you'll pick up all kinds of information—but not if you dominate the conversation. Make it a point to draw out the creative interests and ideas by asking questions. Everybody has an idea or two to give you if you are respectful enough to get that person talking about what he or she does and knows. Draw out the creativity of others at every opportunity. Find out what they are concerned about, what changes they are dealing with in their lives, and what they are interested in. Discover what makes them tick. You'll be surprised how much your own ideas will be influenced by listening to others tell you theirs.

5. Master the Art of the Deep Dive

If you're a scuba diver, you know that a deep dive is one where you descend 55 meters or more. For our purposes, a deep informational dive is one where you descend well below the surface of a topic that is new to you or your organization or department. Say a new topic looms on the horizon. A possible disruption is mentioned for the first time. A competitor introduces a novel bell or whistle that you sense may be significant.

An internal customer sparks your curiosity by asking you a question for which you have no answer. Instead of waiting for somebody else to show initiative, take it upon yourself to develop new working knowledge to think through the implications and examine the possibilities.

There are times when you will be asked to do a deep dive. That was the challenge that Lisa Peters, the human resources maven who orchestrated the Mellon Bank merger with Bank of New York, presented to her transition team. When I interviewed Lisa, she told me how she encouraged her transition teams to discover the *edge*, meaning to benchmark and research "what's best in class out there" and where the trends are going in specialized areas such as benefits, payroll, and human resource practices in general. Instead of outsourcing this learning journey to a consulting firm, Peters challenged various merger teams to do these deep dives themselves.

"What I asked for was an assessment of each of the two merging organizations to determine current best practices. Then I challenged them to do an assessment of what's available on the market, and finally, what do we think is coming down the pike? When you're looking at what's best in the market today, you have to really start talking to companies about what are the innovations that they're going to do next. How are they continuing to change their product and in what time frames? How are they getting information about the future to know what's coming next?"

Mastering the art of the deep dive means paying attention to the changes happening all around you. It means spotting the knowledge deficits that arise in a world of rapid change and being willing to dig up new knowledge to move you ahead.

6. Develop Your Point of View on Key Issues

The Internet is not just the greatest disruptor of all time; it's also an undeniable convenience. With just a few clicks, you can do all sorts of research, whether you're at home, at the office, or in a hotel room. Never has a new communications system changed so many personal habits or played so many roles in our lives.

Technology writer Nicholas Carr is concerned that this easy access to blog posts, videos, podcasts, newspapers, and magazines has a down side. He believes it is chipping away at our capacity for concentration and contemplation. In an *Atlantic Monthly* article, he asks a provocative question: "Is Google Making Us Stupid?"

Not only has the way he reads been altered, but "the way I think has changed," wrote Carr. More and more he finds himself skimming, browsing, bouncing around, and grazing. "My mind now expects to take in information the way the Net distributes it: in a swiftly moving stream of particles.

Once I was a scuba diver in the sea of words. Now I zip along the surface like a guy on a jet ski."

For innovators, Carr raises an important issue. Developing the ability to think ahead of the curve demands more than that we skim and skitter, scan and monitor. It also requires that we ponder what we read. It requires that we take the time to develop our own point of view based on our careful analysis of what we read.

It is this interpretive component on key issues that gives you the edge. Don't allow yourself to succumb to information overload and interpretation underload.

Says Carr: "Our ability to interpret text, to make the rich mental connections that form when we read deeply and without distraction," is what often gets shortchanged by Internet grazing. "The kind of deep reading that a sequence of printed pages promotes is valuable not just for the knowledge we acquire from the author's words but for the intellectual vibrations those words set off within our own minds. In the quiet spaces opened up by sustained, undistracted reading, we make our own associations, draw our own inferences and analogies, and foster our own ideas."

Merely surfing the Net will not give you an edge. Scanning headlines and skimming articles and reports are necessary, but insufficient. Listening to important information, while multitasking away at three other tasks, may seem like a good use of your time, but it will not give you an edge. Reading articles at half or quarter concentration is better than nothing—but not by much.

But if you feed your mind the latest information and ideas and take the time to ponder what it means, you develop a point of view on key issues facing your organization. People will start thinking that you have that rare and highly valued attribute known as vision.

7. Connect the Dots

I ran into *New York Times* columnist Thomas Friedman at a reception in St. Petersburg, Russia, earlier this year. I couldn't help but ask the author of the bestselling book *The World Is Flat* about an expression he'd used when speaking to college students in my town of Santa Barbara. One student asked how to navigate his career in these uncertain times. Tom's answer: Learn to connect the dots.

What are the dots? In his own case, Tom explained how he'd developed expertise in foreign affairs, Washington politics, and business from taking on various assignments and being willing to start from scratch and learn a new area. He urged the students to figure out their "dots" and then find ways to connect their various skill sets to become a more powerful, unique person.

Innovators do this as a matter of routine. They are always learning and looking outside the artificial boundaries that divide departments, professions, industries, and cultures. They always connect the disconnected.

The people who truly see ahead of the curve and change the world are often called visionaries. But, as one of them, FedEx founder Fred Smith, once explained to me, "Vision is just a lot of grinding-it-out information gathering and being willing to make certain assumptions based on the changes that are happening. And sometimes those changes are coming in very different areas and you synthesize them to come up with an idea."

In other words, connect the dots.

8. Give People Permission to Give You Bad News

You've got to give people permission to give you tough news and not shoot the messenger. You must thank people for identifying problems early and giving you the opportunity to solve them. Part of it is the way you handle candid feedback, but the other part is being present.

Listening to bad news the right way can turn a challenging situation into an opportunity to shine.

HOW TO MASTER THIS I-SKILL

Mastering the I-Skill of thinking ahead of the curve requires that you practice every day. It's time to hone this skill into a competitive differentiator for yourself and your firm.

Here are my suggestions for taking action:

1. Monitor trends close at hand. For example, how is your mail changing? What's coming to your physical mailbox these days versus a year or two ago? What are trends in the e-mail you receive?
2. Learn to separate fads from trends. The expression "he/she is always chasing after bright shiny objects" comes to mind. What's the staying power of that new gadget or technology application? Is it a fad?

3. Don't wait for senior management to come to you and explain how they think you and your department can help them invent the future or implement a new culture.
4. Start observing trends and applying them to your life and work with penetrating questions. It won't be long before you come upon fantastic connections that spell opportunity for your organization and for you.

$I-Skill \#5$

Become an Idea Factory

How to Produce an Abundance of Great Ideas Even If You Don't Think You Are Creative

Have you taken your "Doug Day" lately?

I've shared the "Doug Day" method with audiences and clients all over the world. It amazes me how many people respond to this story. One client e-mailed me after a speech to his colleagues gathered in Houston. "After your workshop everyone kept joking about, 'Hey, you need to take a Doug Day. Or a Sylvia Day. Or a Sven Day or a Daniel Day.' Throughout the conference, people kept up the ribbing."

Who is Doug? What is his day? Doug Greene is chairman of New Hope Communications, a fast-growing natural foods company based in Colorado. I asked him where he gets ideas.

"Once a month I schedule what I refer to as a Doug Day," he said. "I create a block of time where I have absolutely nothing to do. I have no appointments; I'll go to another city or to a different environment. And I'll sit and draw or whatever my first instincts are to do. I think about my team. Do we have the right people on the bus and in the right seats? I think about my level of passion and what's going on with my energy level. Am I burning out? Where do I need to make changes? How are we doing against delivering on our strategic plan? I think about opportunities. And I have to say that if I hadn't taken those Doug Days since I started this company, I wouldn't have had nearly the success that we've enjoyed, and I wouldn't have nearly the quality of life."

Imagine how refreshed and rejuvenated you would feel, and how many ideas you might come up with, if you allowed yourself to take a "Doug Day."

Everybody has ideas. But only a few know how to keep their "idea factories" fortified to churn out a wealth of them on a consistent basis, when and where needed, even when the heat is on.

Only a few know how to work with their ideas to solve problems, produce results, and create new opportunities. Only a few know how to deploy their ideas to transform themselves from "competent manager/employee" to "sought-after, difficult-to-replace talent." So this chapter is about developing the innovation skill called Become an Idea Factory, so that you make creativity your value-adding path to indispensability.

SCARCITY CREATES VALUE; VALUE CREATES INDISPENSABILITY

Ever heard somebody say any of the following statements?

"Ideas are not our problem. We have too many compelling ideas around here."

"We generate too many ideas that help cut costs, delight customers, and keep them coming back."

"There are too many ideas that add heft and freshness to our firm's value proposition."

I didn't think so.

The demand for these kinds of ideas is always much greater than the supply, especially today.

Just ask Justin W., who just out of college got hired as an operations management trainee at Nestle's Bloomington, Illinois, factory. It didn't take Justin long before he convinced his managers to allow him to put several cost-cutting ideas of his own invention in place. One idea came about when he found that minor tweaks to packaging and design could make a big difference in reducing waste. Another of his ideas, restacking cases to make room for 10 more on a single pallet, saved the company $60,000 a year. Justin's ideas got him noticed, and he was promoted to supervisor of a team of 20 plant employees.

Not long after, a job opening arose at another company plant in Utah. Justin jumped at the chance. Now he manages 44 hourly workers, some of whom are twice his age. "I was eager to transfer because of the opportunity to gain frontline leadership experience," Justin said.

A scarcity of compelling ideas is what creates value. A scarcity of individuals willing to not only come up with ideas, but to take the necessary steps to implement them, is what creates value.

10 WAYS TO KEEP YOUR IDEA FACTORY HUMMING

If you want to be like Justin W. and Doug Greene and cultivate a never-ending stream of ideas, here are 10 tools to guide you.

---

1. **Inspect your idea factory regularly.**
2. **Identify when and where you do your best thinking.**
3. **Enhance your creative environment.**
4. **Know when to multitask and when to unitask.**
5. **Think of creativity as something you practice, not something you're born with.**
6. **Use your innovation style to your advantage.**
7. **Expand your own methods for getting "unstuck."**
8. **Make the most out of recreation.**
9. **Remember to take your "Doug Day."**
10. **Devise a method for downloading your ideas.**

Let's explore these one by one.

1. Inspect Your Idea Factory Regularly

The quickest, simplest way to check up on your idea factory is to look at your "to do" list. It's a snapshot of the ideas you're working on right now. What does your list reveal? Are the ideas mostly related to your basic functional duties—pick up the dry cleaning, finish crunching the numbers, do x? Or are there also ideas related to larger projects and opportunities and goals from your personal innovation strategy?

Everybody must execute routine details. But if these are the only items on your agenda, your idea factory is greatly in need of retooling. It's not that you aren't generating ideas; you almost certainly are. The problem is that you aren't moving on them in systematic fashion. You are slighting your big ideas while allowing yourself to be overwhelmed by the tactical details. You'll never get ahead this way; at most you'll only get by.

To thoroughly inspect your idea factory, try this for a week: Carry a small notebook wherever you go and jot down ideas as they occur. Examples might be:

- Look into attending social networking seminar sponsored by the marketing department.
- Investigate going back to school to earn MBA.
- Meet with sales department about starting promotional campaign for the new product line.

Checking up on your ideas will make you more aware of the many possibilities that are flashing into your mind. Some will be *lifters*, and some will be *poppers*. The lifters are those you "borrow" from other industries or people—or even from competitors. The poppers are those that come out of your own conjuring process. If you're in the Defeatist Mode or Sustainer Mode when you conjure an idea, you might tune it out. You might reject it the minute it occurs no matter how promising it might be.

Your idea factory requires constant maintenance.

2. Identify When and Where You Do Your Best Thinking
Ask yourself:

- Where are you when you generate your best ideas?
- When, where, and at what time of day do you generally do your best thinking?
- What do you do to get yourself unstuck when facing a vexing problem?
- How did you inject creativity to handle a task in the last 24 hours?
- How often do you come up with solutions that others compliment you on as being "creative"?

Jot down your responses so that you fully explore these issues. If you take time to think about these questions and their answers, you'll gain further insight into your own ways of fortifying your idea factory. The next step is to go to that space when you want to do some serious cogitating.

If there's a time of day when you feel you do your most creative thinking, try to reserve it for yourself and use it to its fullest. If there's a particular spot that says "idea space" to you—your study or the bathtub—set aside time to use that space, alone and free of noise and distraction. Check out places outside your home, too: a park, a library, even a reasonably quiet coffee shop. Find a place where you feel safe to think and dream.

3. Enhance Your Creative Environment

Not long ago, I worked on a major project with Rinaldo Brutoco, founder and CEO of US Television, one of the pioneers of cable television in the 1970s. Brutoco went on to co-found the World Business Academy with Stanford University social scientist Willis Harmon. For a creative thinking session, the Brutocos invited my wife and me to join them at their vacation home in Hawaii. Since this was to be a short working vacation, I assumed we'd be eating out. But right after we arrived, Brutoco suggested that we head to the supermarket.

Once there, Rinaldo began filling the cart as if he hadn't eaten in days. Bottles of juices, fresh pineapples and other island fruits, exotic cheeses and spreads—the bill came to several hundred dollars. I asked him who all the food was for. "Us!" he exclaimed. Back at his home, we began working, ideas began flowing, and the time flew. The wisdom behind his extravagance was soon evident. If we'd gone out for lunch every day, we might have lost momentum. Instead, while snacking on healthy foods, we were able to cover a lot of ground each day and still knock off in the late afternoons to join our wives for some fun.

Brutoco was consciously enhancing our creative environment. But you don't have to spend hundreds of dollars or fly to Hawaii to enhance yours. In fact, you can do things to your office to turn it into a better place to brainstorm ideas.

Others find their inspiration out of the office. Wayne Silby, the financial services innovator, favors floating in his isolation tank to "see what bubbles up." For one engineer at a defense industry company, many of his best ideas come to him when he gets up early and goes into his study to listen to classical music. You may find you will get a surprising number of new ideas when you are working hard on an unrelated project.

Let creativity flow to you inside and outside your office.

4. Know When to Multitask and When to Unitask

Imagine that you are in Florence, Italy, on a business trip. The work part of the trip is over. You head over to the Galleria dell'Accademia to view Michelangelo's *David*.

You think about the focus and skill of the sculptor who produced this great work. Then your mobile phone rings, breaking the spell, and you find yourself in a call with somebody on another continent. You move away from the crowd because you must "take this important call." When you return to the greatest sculpture on the planet you find yourself imagining Michelangelo chipping away at the marble with a mobile phone scrunched up to his ear—multitasking. Hardly.

You and I may think we're more productive when we work on multiple tasks at once, but research shows otherwise.

Stanford University Professor Clifford Nass concludes that "multitaskers were just lousy at everything." He and his researchers found that, compared with non-multitaskers, multitaskers performed poorly on a variety of tasks, were easily distracted, and had difficulty focusing.

"The core of the problem," Nass says, "[is that multi-taskers] think they're great at what they do. They've convinced everybody else that they're good at it, too."

It's a challenge to cut out multitasking when creative concentration would serve us better. We all get a sense of being productive from being able to keep several balls in the air at once. Everyone enjoys crossing items off that "to do" list.

What I recommend is this: If you're doing routine work, multitask till your heart is content! But when you're doing important work, make it a point not to multitask.

Work on one project at a time. Don't answer your phone. Close all web browsers and eliminate distractions. And unitask—meaning that you work on one task at a time. Even when your thoughts wander, or you do get sidetracked, remind yourself of the importance of focusing singularly rather than scattering your mental force across multiple issues.

Michelangelo didn't multitask when he was in full creative mode. Neither should you.

5. Think of Creativity as Something You Practice, Not Something You're Born With

Every morning at 5:30, choreographer Twyla Tharp rolls out of bed, dons a leotard, and hails a cab over to a New York City gym for a two-hour workout.

In her 35-year career, she's created 130 dances and ballets and numerous hit shows on Broadway. She's worked with dancers, set designers, and musicians in the opera houses of London, Paris, Stockholm, Sydney, and Berlin. She's run her own company for three decades. And all the while she has adhered to the discipline of early morning exercise to fire her creative imagination.

Tharp gathered her insights on the creative process into a fascinating book, *The Creative Habit: Learn It and Use It for Life.* Creativity, observes Tharp, is not a gift from the gods but the result of preparation, routine, effort, and discipline. Most important, it's within the reach of everyone who wants to try to tap it. Creativity isn't for just artists, it's "for businesspeople looking for a new way to close a sale; it's for engineers trying to solve a problem; for parents who want their children to excel, and who know that their creativity will be what differentiates."

What should a person do who wants to perform at peak creative levels? Tharp suggests establishing creative routines. "The routine is as much a part of the creative process as the lightning bolt of inspiration, maybe more; and the routine is available to everyone."

More than anything, her years of output point to the value of preparation. Tharp admits that there's a paradox in the notion that creativity should be thought of as springing from a habit. "We think of creativity as a way of keeping everything fresh and new, while habit implies routine and repetition. That paradox intrigues me because it occupies the place where creativity and skill rub up against each other. . . ."

"No one can give you your subject matter, your creative content," she concludes. "If they could, it would be their creation and not yours. But there's a process that generates creativity—and you can learn it. You can make it habitual."

The world may not notice if you don't exercise your imagination today, tomorrow, or the next day. But you will. In the rush of day-to-day tactical execution, not adhering to creative routines may result in atrophied creative muscles. The less you write, think, or create, the harder they are to do.

The more you create, the more creative you become.

6. Use Your Innovation Style to Your Advantage

Sir Ken Robinson, author of *Why Schools Kill Creativity* and a tireless advocate for nurturing creativity in kids, tells the story of the teacher who handed out paint and brushes and protective gear to her little charges and turned them loose. Paint anything you want, she invited them. As she visited her pupils, she asked a child what she was painting. "I'm painting a picture of God," said the girl matter-of-factly.

"But nobody knows what God looks like."

"They will when I'm finished," said the child.

As children, none of us define ourselves as being uncreative. As adults, most of us define creativity as what creative people do, and we leave ourselves on the sidelines. The conclusion of virtually every expert who has studied creativity challenges this assumption. For example, William Miller, whose four innovation styles were summarized earlier, suggests that the question of "Are you creative?" is the wrong question. Instead, "How are you creative?" is more helpful to understand if we are to use our preferred innovation style to our advantage. Each of Miller's four basic styles contains inherent strengths and potential Achilles heels when it comes to getting new projects done. For example:

Visioning Style: If this is your preferred style, you don't have a problem coming up with ideas; that part is easy. You produce ideas having to do with "the way it could be but isn't now" at the drop of a hat. The downside of this style is that you can tend to be unrealistic about the details and the action plans and the follow-through involved in turning vision into reality. To make this style work for you, it's necessary to partner with those of other styles to maximize results and avoid becoming a dreamer, not a doer.

Modifying Style: If you prefer this style, you are apt to think of yourself as not being creative and thereby discount your contribution. Your strength is your discipline and attention to detail, your ability to streamline work and come up with countless ways to simplify processes. You are most comfortable discovering solutions that have worked in the past. But when there's no real history to draw from (as is often the case when the task at hand is unconventional), or when there's a great deal of uncertainty, you tend to chafe. This can lead you to want to think small, instead of boldly, and you can tend to sit on those of the visioning style. In these situations, you want to collaborate and give wide berth to those you may consider wacky, and team up with those of the exploring and visioning styles to embrace possibilities that may even frighten you a bit in their boldness. You need to remind yourself to assault your assumptions, especially when your firm is facing disruption in the marketplace.

Exploring Style: If this is your preferred style, you're probably very intuitive, and you are great at turning "conventional wisdom" on its head. Like the visionaries, coming up with ideas is easy for you. Your enthusiasm for launching off in new directions is boundless. But

136

you chafe when the structure for how work is organized gets too tight or when your team needs to get down to the basics of project planning and execution. To make this style work for you, it is necessary to honor folks of other styles and help them unleash their best efforts; otherwise your natural tendencies can detract from your overall performance.

Experimenting Style: If you like facts, working models, and experimentation, chances are this is your preferred style of innovating. Your value-adding advantage is that once a common process or approach to understanding a situation is established, you can troubleshoot just about anything. Your contribution to groups is your systematic, thorough evaluation of new ideas and your uncanny ability to build consensus for practical solutions. But you can get caught up in overtesting and overanalyzing, and you can be reluctant to take calculated risks. You can become an expert on all the ways that don't work, but bureaucratic-prone and cautious to a fault. To make this style work for you, start consciously taking more risks in your life.

As Plato said centuries ago, "Know thyself." And know your preferred innovation style. Then use it to your advantage rather than allowing it to be a limiting factor.

7. Expand Your Own Methods for Getting "Unstuck"

When you're working on a huge problem or trying to actualize a significant opportunity, you'll probably get stuck somewhere along the way.

One of the more creative entrepreneurs I know described how easy it is to go from "flow state" to "shut down."

"What I do is mentally move up above myself and observe myself creating—literally popping out ideas like popcorn over a hot fire. I observe myself reacting and building on the flow and the love you feel for yourself and the streaming, and the way my inner voice is saying, 'okay this is going great, I'm feeling the flow, life is great, pop, here's an idea on that [marketing] issue and boom here's an idea for the Monday morning meeting and, yes, we could do this, we will do that.' Then suddenly, I've freaked out, I've shut down, I can't think, lost my thought, where was I, I can't . . . oh, yeah, that old issue just popped up on the radar, or I glanced over at my phone (which was on vibrate, but still) and couldn't help but see the bit of bad news that came in on a text message. What thoughts am I having that are shutting my creativity down? What person did I interact with whose negative words came suddenly to the surface?

"You have to figure out what's charging your batteries, what's giving you that juice, that jolt, that electricity of belief, belief that you can, will, etc., and you have to figure out what's creating the pull or the drag. Start by identifying how you're reacting, because basically all you have to work with is yourself.

"Once I learned what those things were, I started avoiding them. Anything that drains my energy or shuts me down, I try to manage."

One way to get back on track is just to stop, acknowledge that you are stuck, and shift.

"When I get stuck," one engineer told me, "I walk out and clear my head and then query somebody on the idea. This isn't easy at my company because I have to find someone with two attributes: (1) enough technical knowledge base to understand what I'm talking about and (2) a mind open enough to hear something that is not completely thought out."

Most people I've queried on this issue report that their best thinking is done "alone and undistracted." They prefer to do their own thinking first, then find sharing with a larger group a good way of expanding the idea. Other methods include:

"If I need to get unstuck, I go work on something else and eventually an answer comes to me."

"If stuck, I'll explore related interests (design and architecture). I'll talk with creative friends in other fields to hear about what they're working on or ask them to respond to my challenge. I might go to a museum."

"If stuck, I either go for a walk or talk out loud or I work at my white board or sketch pad to think 'on paper.' If I'm still stuck, I switch to another task and allow the first one to gel in the background for a while."

"If stuck, I move on to something else, and come back to [the problem] after the previous ideas are no longer in my mind."

"I talk to other experts. Our company is very good at having older experts who are willing to talk to you and share a great deal of advice."

"I'll put it aside, take a walk, visit a hobby store, or sleep on it.
I often awake in the night with complete solutions. I keep
paper and pencil next to bed (and in car) at all times."

"I will call a group session or take time away from work to
get a fresh perspective."

"I narrow the problem and focus on a smaller issue/aspect
to generate ideas."

"To get unstuck, I reach out to colleagues . . . run ideas by
them. I also flip through books or find web sites that
describe different processes that align with what I'm trying
to create."

"If stuck, I try to bounce the problem off others, thinking
out loud. This always worked for me when I used to do
software development."

"I'll focus on something else for awhile (a day or two), then
come up with an answer."

"When I get really stuck, I walk away—literally. [I] find it helpful to leave whatever workspace I'm in, walk around a bit,
leave the task, let it marinate, then go back to it. Mostly
being stuck and getting unstuck is all part of the process—
it doesn't scare me like it did when I was younger."

There are lots of different ways to get unstuck. Use the
one that works for you.

8. Make the Most Out of Recreation

For eight glorious days several summers ago, 23 compan-
ions and I rafted down the Colorado River through the
Grand Canyon. Each day our eyes feasted on some of
the most beautiful scenery on Earth—when we weren't

hanging on for dear life as we shot endless rapids, getting slammed by six-foot-high barrages of ice cold, gritty, muddy river water.

In the evenings, we enjoyed tasty meals prepared by our four professional guides. Over delicious wines, we talked over and laughed about the events of the day. Thinking about business began to recede from the epicenter of my thoughts. The most amazing thing happened when I realized that I could live without my iPhone and that my staff could carry on without me. I arrived back in civilization with a renewed sense of joy in the work that I do and a new perspective on the importance of recreation—getting totally away from the work.

If you're connected electronically, you're also connected mentally and psychologically. You're working problems; you're worrying over decisions and relationships and managing from afar. Those left in charge really aren't in charge. You may be physically with your family and friends on safari in Botswana, but metabolically you're back at the office. Once your mind reenters the familiar realm of work, the competitive juices course through your body and you crowd out the very dream space that leisure can provide.

Even with all the long hours workers rack up, they are not anxious to delegate, disconnect, and disappear. Various strategies show a growing trend toward blurring vacations into an extension of the regular grind. One in five executives now take along their laptops on vacation and eight in ten, their mobile phones.

Here's the problem. Unless you establish personal guidelines for the time out of the office, you never really pause to alter consciousness to think about what it all means. This is what vacations are for. So:

1. If you must connect with your office, do so only once a day. Ask an assistant or colleague to make a list of the critical things to be discussed. Be brief and be off.

2. Make a list of books you want to read on vacation well in advance. The right book can transform a mediocre vacation into a great one.

3. Figure out whether your vacation should be active and adventuresome or more sedentary and calm, based on the kind of schedule you've been keeping of late. If you've had a tumultuous schedule, allow yourself to be lazy, directionless, and spontaneous. If you're up for an adventure, I recommend the Colorado River.

4. Commit to being "in the moment." Only you know your thoughts, so only you will know if you're thinking about business. As with meditation, when you realize you're focusing on the chatter in your mind, you don't give up, you just get back on track.

5. Fuel your creative spirit by getting plenty of exercise, treating yourself to a massage, listening to music, and taking an adventure vacation at least once in a while.

6. Keep a journal on your vacation. Record not only what you see and what you experience but how you feel.

7. If you can't take an extended getaway this year, take periodic, short mini-vacations. They're better than nothing. If you don't allow yourself to disconnect, you won't be able to recreate.

9. Remember to Take Your "Doug Day"

One attendee of my Innovative Thinking seminars wrote to tell me how he'd rented a convertible and was driving up the Pacific Northwest on an extended Doug Day. If you decide to try out this method, notice what he did. He unplugged with no gadgets to tempt him to "check in with the office." He didn't keep a schedule. Time was not his driver. Intuition-driven, he was out there to think. He invited his mind to tune in to the ideas that might bubble up. Stepping back, he captured them.

10. Devise a Method for Downloading Your Ideas

If you took a video camera in hand and followed around some of the world's leading innovators, one habit you would find them engaging in is writing down their ideas when they occur and capturing them in enough detail to recall them later. I first noticed this habit in the early 1980s in a study of the personal best practices of prominent American innovators that became the book *Winning the Innovation Game.* Sure, the methods of downloading have changed since then. Today you can call yourself and leave a lengthy voicemail full of hot ideas. You can speak them into a digital recorder or your smartphone. Or you can jot them down on sticky notes at your desk or on a small pad.

The real trick, the discipline if you will, is to get into the habit of downloading your ideas wherever and whenever you hatch them. If you don't capture an idea the moment it strikes, you're unlikely to act on it later. The mind is a terrific instrument for coming up with ideas, but an equally terrible storage device for them.

When you are "on a roll" and the ideas start popping, take action. The simple act of capturing your ideas in a permanent place frees your mind to generate even more. And as has often been said, to have a good idea, have lots of them.

Famous innovators often keep idea notebooks or journals for working with their ideas—for fleshing them out. Edison, da Vinci, Twain, van der Rohe, and many others regarded their notebooks as vital tools. They used them as spaces to let go, for freeform sketches or word pictures, to doodle, to be childlike, to grab primitive imaginings and figments.

Capture your ideas before they fly away.

HOW TO MASTER THIS I-SKILL

As Jonas Salk, Twyla Tharp, and countless other innovators have discovered, hatching the ideas you need to power your life and build your career is the result of a habit, a personal best practice. By looking at your brain as your idea factory, you begin to tune in to ways you can fortify that output machine rather than passively waiting for ideas to come, or hoping somebody comes up with the ideas for you. They won't.

Mastering the I-Skill of Becoming an Idea Factory begins with realizing that just doing your job is not enough. What will differentiate you is the quality and quantity of your ideas directed at adding value to the teams you collaborate on, the boss you serve, and the department you work within. Ideas are your product. They are your ticket to indispensability. So by all means:

1. Take the time to inspect your idea factory now before moving on to the next chapter. Do it now and periodically in the months and years ahead. Look not just at the ideas you're generating, but at what is happening with those ideas. If you've gotten bogged down by the minutia of tactical execution, shift consciously into Innovator Mode. Reread your personal innovation strategy and coax yourself to come up with ideas to move you forward.

2. Become conscious of when an issue you must deal with, a decision you must make, or an opportunity you wish to maximize would benefit from unitasking.

3. Know yourself in terms of the time of day and the specific locations that often produce a flood of ideas.

4. Do plan to take a Doug Day. Put it on the calendar and take it seriously. You'll find that it rejuvenates you for the work you do and the projects you contribute to.

If you've paused long enough to consider the suggestions in this chapter, you'll have a good sense of how your idea factory has been functioning, and you'll have some new tools to help you determine where you want to make changes going forward. And you'll also be ready to tackle the next innovation skill with gusto—becoming a high-demand collaborator!

$I-Skill \# 6$

Become a Standout Collaborator

Galvanize Teams and Departments to Get New Initiatives Done

"Never forget that a small group of committed citizens can change the world," said Margaret Mead, the renowned anthropologist. "Indeed, it's the only thing that ever has."

One woman who changed the world, or at least the destiny of her company, was Nancy Snyder of Whirlpool, whom we first met in the I-Skill #2 chapter. At the time, the Michigan-based appliance manufacturer faced the forces of a major disruption. Not a fast-erupting storm, it was more of a slow unraveling of its business model. Its major products—dishwashers, washers, and dryers—were becoming a commodity, and prices were dropping at the rate of 3.4 percent a year. Its stock price was stuck. Growth had stalled. Whirlpool customers were not loyal to brand and the company was entering a recession.

Chief executive officer (CEO) Dave Whitwam was aware of these issues, and he had a sudden epiphany while visiting an appliance store. "I've got pretty good eyesight," he recalled. "But as I looked at a row of washers, even I couldn't tell ours from the competition." Whitwam knew his company had to transform itself, and he believed a fundamentally new approach to innovation was required.

Soon thereafter, Whitwam tapped an obscure organization development specialist to help him radically transform Whirlpool Corporation. His goal for the company: Embed innovation into every job. The new motto became: "Innovation from everyone and everywhere." Creating a range of exciting new products that customers would notice became everyone's responsibility.

In the ensuing years, Whirlpool's innovation program became a role model for many other companies to benchmark. Snyder went on to be interviewed in *Business Week* and other publications and wrote two books that documented Whirlpool's journey; today, she teaches a course in innovation at the University of Notre Dame.

When I asked Nancy what she considers the most essential I-Skill of them all, she didn't hesitate. "Figure out how to work in teams," she said. "If you're not a good team player, you can't innovate. At Whirlpool, it takes hundreds of people working in teams to get an innovation to market. If you think you're going to be the loner, or you're going to be the star, it's just not going to work."

Nancy speaks from long experience. Even if you're a genius in your area of expertise, you'll never achieve your

148

potential if your collaboration skills are lacking, and you'll never become indispensible. Your company may need to keep you around because nobody else can do what you do. But don't count on this "expertise monopoly" lasting. Sooner or later, your firm will find ways to bust up that monopoly— and you could be looking for a job.

To collaborate is "to work together, especially in a joint intellectual effort." Although hierarchies remain in place in most 21st century organizations, collaborative teams are how big projects actually get done. And that's where the I-Skill of becoming a standout collaborator comes in handy.

THE WRIGHT WAY TO COLLABORATE

Will Wright is developer of The Sims, Spore, and other best-selling computer games. Wright was asked what it takes to produce such unusual products. His answer: talent and team-work ability.

"You can have a great person who doesn't really work well on the team, and they're a net loss," Wright told *New York Times* columnist Adam Bryant. "You can have somebody who is not that great, but they are really very good glue, so that could be a net gain."

Wright separates people into two basic groups: glue and solvents. "Team members I consider glue disseminate things effectively, motivate, and improve morale. They basically bring the team tighter and tighter. Solvents, on the other hand, are more of an energy drain. It's just their personal nature that they might be disagreeable. They rub people the wrong way. They're always caught in conflicts.

"Occasionally I will get somebody who is more of a prima donna, who is just incredibly good, but not great on the team and so, in some ways, you can find a role where you can kind of isolate and quarantine them and allow them to go off and do their great work without having to interact with the rest of the team a lot. Those people are fairly few and far between."

"How do you glean that from an interview?" Wright was asked.

"That part is very hard to get from an interview," said Wright. "A lot of times you can subtly kind of push back on things they are saying and find out if they are argumentative, or do they tend to take the conversation in a constructive direction? Their self-image relative to what other people have said about them is really interesting to me. When you call their references, if there is a very big discrepancy between their self-image and what other people are saying about them, that is usually indicative of some underlying kind of social issue you are going to be facing down the road. On the other hand, if they come and they are underselling themselves and you talk to everybody they worked with and they are telling you they're a superstar, then usually that indicates that they are going to [be] an added benefit in the team setting."

As Will Wright has discovered, native talent is not enough. It can be a net loss if your ability to work with others is left underdeveloped.

COLLABORATION'S PAYOFF: THE THREE Rs

When you contribute successfully to teams and work groups, you'll be rewarded in three ways. I call them the three Rs:

Result: You are part of a mission accomplished, a "success episode." You have a story to tell and a track record to support you.

Reputation: Your stature in the organization rises. Your boss is happy, and your colleagues talk you up, praise your contribution, and invite you to join them in future projects.

Residuals: Your satisfaction after the project is completed is what this final R is all about. The lasting payout of participating in a successful collaboration is that you get to see your "product" being used by customers, both internal and external. You know you've made a difference, solved a problem, or created an opportunity for the organization, your team, or department. Most of all, you know you were a standout collaborator.

12 WAYS TO BECOME A STANDOUT COLLABORATOR

If you want to build your collaboration skills to be more like those of a Nancy Snyder or a Will Wright, you can. It's a matter of becoming more conscious of how you're showing up and mastering 12 critical techniques. They are:

---

1. **Seek to be invited to participate on special project teams.**

2. **Identify what good collaboration looks like.**

3. **Know what bad collaboration feels like.**

4. **Unleash your inner collaborator.**

(continued)

---

5. Become an energizer and not an energy drain.
6. Lead collaboratively.
7. Figure out the right size for your team.
8. Give thought to team composition.
9. Invite people to join you.
10. Recruit people who have a track record of results.
11. Launch your project team right.
12. Establish a group process.

1. Seek to Be Invited to Participate on Special Project Teams

Not everybody aspires to be a collaboration champion. But don't conclude prematurely that you don't have the right stuff or that you can't master this unique art form. With experience, you can. And participating successfully on collaborative teams is the quickest route to becoming an in-demand associate in your firm.

The first objective is getting invited to participate in special project teams. The second is performing on every team you get invited to join in such a way that you exceed expectations.

How can you maneuver yourself and your career toward high-visibility projects, given that most will be in addition to your regular workload? One way to start is by getting appointed to teams that are chartered to do something outside the confines of your department. By serving on them, you are afforded the opportunity to grow skills, push beyond your prior limits, and interact with some of the smartest people in your firm.

How do you hear about such projects? By building your internal network, keeping your ear to the ground, and exhibiting an opportunity mindset.

2. Identify What Good Collaboration Looks Like

I love observing great collaborative teams at work. Some people enjoy observing great stage performers, master craftsmen, musicians, and sports figures perform. I enjoy watching effective teams coming together, coalescing as a group, making progress, working through problems and setbacks, and ultimately getting new things done.

They make it look effortless. They inspire laughter and have fun. There is a spirit of adventure.

When you peer closely at effective collaborators at work, you find somebody in a leadership role who understands motivation and the need to keep everyone focused on the goal. Collaborating on a project is a journey. Like all journeys, there will be twists and turns, ups and downs, good days and bad days.

Effective collaboration is the result of having a clearly defined goal. If the goal is a stretch, if it requires figuring something out that has never been done before, the journey can be exhilarating.

Effective collaboration requires sharing information and constant give-and-take. It requires constructive, no-holds-barred giving and receiving of feedback. It means coming to the aid of another person on the team when that person is faltering.

Good collaboration is the result of trust.

3. Know What Bad Collaboration Feels Like

Bad collaboration has a distinctive feel. You dread associating with the group. You become anxious rather than excited. You find yourself avoiding your colleagues; you feel fear in the pit of your stomach. Bad collaboration occurs when there is a lack of trust, a lack of leadership, and a lack of clearly defined goals. People hoard information, using it as a jockeying tool to gain power and control. They try to make themselves look good and others incompetent. They discredit and blame. They play games and posture.

An assignment to assist a government agency in Washington comes to mind. (I've radically changed the details of this example to protect my client, even though it is a governmental agency.) When my colleague and I at The Innovation Resource Consulting Group entered the picture, the team had already been flailing around for more than a year, attempting to develop an idea management program for the agency's 200,000 employees. The three de facto leaders of this initiative were barely on speaking terms, and their communication was minimal.

Meetings were a competition to see who could utter the most jargon-laden sentences. Revealing certain facts with an arch tone of, "Well if you were in the loop, you'd know that . . ." was a way of subtly scoring points. Individual status was conveyed to those around the table through position and power, and the pecking order overshadowed and intimidated the team's work.

The core team was a loose affiliation of leaderless specialists, none of whom appeared to know the first thing about innovation or had exhibited any curiosity about the subject. This lack of knowledge did not dissuade them in the least.

The most shocking thing about the project was the lack of clearly defined objectives. Vague targets were alluded to from time to time. But it was obvious that meeting deadlines and being held accountable were not of great concern. The team was three or four times as large as a private company would have assigned to the task, and "membership" on the project team was ill defined.

I doubt the issue of membership status even crossed anyone's mind. I doubt that most people who appeared to be key players really believed they were official members of the team. Instead, key people seemed to be only serial contributors with slightly greater responsibility but a noticeable lack of urgency or accountability. Everything just lumbered along, and this was but one of any number of vague projects and teams and endless meetings they participated in during the course of their work.

The only time I saw this roving band of miscollaborators get serious about a deadline was when they had a date to discuss their project with the secretary, a member of President Bush's cabinet and their ultimate boss. Preparing for the briefing consumed several months. Briefing day itself was reminiscent of what it must have been like to have been granted an audience with an 18th-century European king.

Each of the 30 or so workers (several of whom told me that in their long careers at the agency, they had never laid eyes on a secretary) was dressed in their Sunday finest. Just before we entered the dimly lit wood-paneled boardroom, we were instructed not to chew gum or take water bottles with us. We were to remain standing until the secretary arrived and was seated. As I looked around the room at these suddenly serious bureaucrats, two thoughts crossed my mind: "This guy doesn't have the foggiest notion of what is actually going on with this project team" and "There's got to be a better way."

"These presentation slides have been vetted by dozens of people," announced one of the presenters, as she launched into her remarks. This was an understatement.

After the briefing was deemed an unqualified success, it was decided that an offsite event involving anyone from the field who wanted to accelerate progress would be the best way to get the innovation process designed and up and running. My colleague and I were tasked with helping organize the offsite event, which was to take place far from headquarters in Washington.

In the ensuing weeks, a swarm of e-mails buzzed about. Everyone piped in with their opinions, nobody in charge, yet with anyone and everyone apparently exhibiting veto power as consensus was sought. The crabbiest and crustiest among those participating seemed to wield power over the course of decisions. Among the decisions that seemed to weigh heaviest were (1) Could we hold an opening dinner to get everyone on the same page? and (2) If so, could we serve alcohol?

Bad collaboration is the result of poorly defined goals.

4. Unleash Your Inner Collaborator

All standout collaborators share specific attitudes:

- *Exhibit selfless behavior.* "If people perceive that you have a personal agenda, forget about progress," said one worker we interviewed. "You've always got to be mindful of how your actions will be viewed. You've always got to couch things as, 'Here's what could be in your best interest and for the company.' If I have a secret sauce, I think it would be, 'How do I encourage others to call this idea or approach their own?'"
- *Inspire trust.* To be perceived as someone who can be trusted is to be able to inspire trust in others. "Trust is the lubrication that makes it possible for organizations to work," notes Warren Bennis. In Chapter 3, I asked you to try to determine the level of trust within your organization, functional department, or work group. The issue of trust comes up as soon as the team is formed. You look around and ask yourself, "Whom do I trust, and whom do I not trust?" Most times, I'm sorry to say, you end up with a calculation that yells to your inner voice: "Proceed with caution. Go slow. Watch so and so for signs of self-dealing." You inspire trust when you are trustworthy, when you do what you say you'll do, when you've promised. When you do these acts you build a track record. Trust, like china or crystal, is easily broken.
- *Be all about service.* This doesn't mean only customer service, but service to others and to the team or work group. You help bring out the best in others. You lend a hand when, for example, you notice somebody on the

157

team struggling or not participating fully. When you're in a service mindset, you've submerged your ego. It's often the little things that reveal this approach.

Your inner collaborator is the best contributor you can be.

5. Be an Energizer and Not an Energy Drain

In *The Hidden Power of Social Networks*, Rob Cross and Andrew Parker describe their efforts to define the characteristics of high-performing employees. They expected to find that the best problem solvers would be those who were most effective at finding the right information. But they also tested another theory.

They examined the "energy network" of an organization and uncovered a rather unexpected quality of high performers; they were able to convince and enthuse others about their ideas. Not only were these "energizers" better performers, but they also raised the performance of others who worked closely with them.

"Good or at least feasible ideas are abundant in organizations," Cross and Parker write, "but having an epiphany is no big deal unless you can motivate others to believe in it and act on it. Energizers are better at getting others to act on their ideas within organizations."

De-energizers, according to these researchers, are often unable to find ways to value other people's perspectives and persist in ineffective approaches instead of trying new ways to engage the group. Energizers, on the other hand, create opportunities for people to enter conversations or problem-solving sessions in ways that make them feel heard.

"They are not blinded by their own thoughts, perspectives, or points of view," write Cross and Parker.

Furthermore, energizers put themselves at an advantage by attracting other high performers. "Reputation spreads quickly," Cross and Parker conclude, "and people position themselves to work for those who are engaging."

When you perform well you inspire others to do the same.

6. Lead Collaboratively

The demands of your "day job" can often cause you to neglect team-building demands, which are constant. If you're the team leader, count on the coordinating, handholding details and endless ("just a quick question . . .") e-mails taking up more time than you thought. Make time at regular intervals to review your team's mission statement and time line and to think at length about how each person is getting along and performing. A team is on a journey, and the environment it is passing through is constantly changing. You, as the leader, add indispensable value when you step back and consider these big picture issues. Seek to convey the desire for, and the commitment to, the team spirit that happens in a close-knit family.

If you're fortunate enough to be asked to lead a collaborative team, this is a breakthrough. My suggestion is to grab your pen and paper, head away from your office, and do some strategizing and planning. Preparation for team success is vital, and this means thinking through who should be chosen for the team, what the right size of the team should be, what the group culture should be, and how you as the leader can maximize the probability of success.

Team spirit is like being in a close-knit family.

7. Figure Out the Right Size for Your Team

A veteran collaborator put the issue of team size this way. "I'm an introvert," he told me. "When the group gets to be over about five people, I find myself starting to shut down, check out, not listen. But under that number, I'm fine, I'm engaged, it's okay."

Figuring out the right size of a team you are forming is definitely worth contemplating. The larger the team, the more coordinating work is necessary. I've heard that the amount of communication needed to coordinate a tiger team rises geometrically with the size of the team. An eight-person team requires 87 percent more communication than a six-person team. That means that beyond a certain size (usually from 5 to 7), each added member may increase the team's coordination time nearly as much as its productive time. That is why a team of 12 or 14 may end up being less productive than a team of 5 or 6. Also keep in mind that in a typical collaborative team, each member has direct access to every other, including the leader.

Perhaps the most important reason for keeping teams somewhere in the magic sweet spot of 5 to 7 is that with larger teams, you lose accountability and productivity. "By the time you get up to eight or nine people [on a team]," observes Katherine J. Klein, professor of management at the Wharton School, "it is cumbersome and you will have a team that breaks down into sub-teams . . . [A]s a team gets larger, there is a tendency for social loafing, where someone gets to slide, to hide."

In teams, more is not always better.

8. Give Thought to Team Composition

Becoming a standout collaborator involves being able to meld diverse personalities, innovation styles, expertise, education levels, and cultural backgrounds into a highly functioning, motivated, united team. There are two theories on the issue of team diversity.

One theory is that people perform best when working with people they like, and we tend to like people who are like us. This would suggest that visioning types work best with visioning types, and modifiers would best be teamed with modifiers.

Another school of thought says: "Hey, we're trying to innovate here! If we all think alike, only one of us is necessary."

So combining diverse points of view and styles of thinking and joining "I've seen it all" old-timers with "Why can't we do it this way" young bucks are effective strategies. Different ages, genders, cultural backgrounds, and innovation styles can form a stronger mix. The downside is that diversity can lead to conflict and poor social integration with poor leadership.

In their research, Klein and Beng-Chong Lim, a profes sor at Nanyang Business School, Nanyang Technological University, Singapore, describe how "team mental models"— defined as a group's shared, organized understanding and mental representation of knowledge about key elements of the team's relevant environment—may enhance coordination and effectiveness in performing tasks that are complex, unpredictable, urgent, and/or novel. Team members who share similar mental models can, these authors suggest, "anticipate each other's responses and coordinate effectively when time is of the essence and opportunities for overt communication and debate are limited."

My own conclusion is this: Recruit diverse personalities or recruit like personalities based on the nature of the challenge. If you're going to be doing some pioneering, you need some visioning folks on board, because they are the source of powerful ideas. And if the team is tasked with implementing the vision, you need implementers.

But the bigger rule of thumb is this: Refuse to stock your team with gamesmen, neurotics, those who are easily agitated, self-centered narcissists, backbiters, gossipers, slackers, jerks, and/or ill-tempered people. Avoid them like the plague. If you have to go outside your team for ideas, do it. If you short-change the value of their longevity because you refuse to invite the just-about-to retire, "I can tell you 10 reasons this idea won't work" veterans, so be it. Just invite feedback from outsiders of this persuasion and realize they are out there, waiting for the chance to toss cold water on your plan.

The right team mix yields the right outcome.

9. Invite People to Join You

Ever notice how a written invitation to a party or social function gets your attention? It puts you in an expectant mood. You are sure to enter it into your calendar, and you show up ready to have fun. This is why the way you invite people to join your team is so important. You establish a vibe. You flatter people and build them up when you tell them why you think they'd be good and what they're likely to get out of it.

Try like crazy to avoid allowing other people to appoint members to be on your team. Tell them that since you are ultimately responsible for the results, that you'd rather be the recruiter. This might raise eyebrows, but right away it shows you are thinking and that you're driving toward results with eyes wide open. No deadwood. No, "We'd better invite [so and so] because of [this or that lame, inadequate excuse]." Gently, but firmly, explain your reasons for being the "decider" and stick to your guns. Down the road, you'll be glad you did.

You're in charge, so take charge, right from the beginning.

10. Recruit People Who Have a Track Record of Results

And be sure to recruit people who have a good track record. Your team may do great work, but if your ideas are not accepted "upstairs" because of "politics," all is for naught. You may want to pioneer, to cover some new ground—in other words, your team wants to penetrate a new market, do x or y. Be sure to attract well-placed folks to your team.

11. Launch Your Project Team Right

I once was invited to serve on the board of directors for a distance learning university. The president who invited me to join had read my books and invited me to lunch at the university club. He couldn't have been more gracious.

I was once invited to join the board of a private school my daughter attended and still remember my first board

163

meeting. I wasn't welcomed, nobody came over to shake my hand, the board president barely acknowledged me at all. From that cold beginning, I found I dreaded serving on that board. I looked forward to its meetings like dental work.

The important contrast I took away from serving on these two teams is that establishing good initial chemistry means everything. Good chemistry doesn't just happen; it's the result of thoughtful leadership and selfless behavior. Members of a team will size each other up, taking measure. If you attune yourself to these matters of respecting others, being polite, and exhibiting proper manners, you'll distinguish yourself right out of the box and set a tone of collegiality that will raise the level of your entire team's work for the duration. People will want to come to your meetings. They'll return your phone calls. They will view you as an indispensable asset.

Treat group members the way you like to be treated.

12. Establish a Group Process

Lack of group process is another collaboration killer. It's very hard for a group of people to get in a room without any team process and try to innovate. Even veteran collaborator Nancy Snyder was no match for "lack of group process" when invited to join an ad hoc team outside Whirlpool.

"Even after all the experience I've had at Whirlpool," recalls Snyder, "I remember being invited to participate in solving a very big problem that the government was facing. They brought a group of people in from all over the world to help them brainstorm. They spent a lot of money to have us help them, put us in a room with all these gizmos, and said, 'Okay, think hard.' Well, we didn't know each other. We didn't have a group process, and we just couldn't do it. So I think part of it is, if your company doesn't have one, create one. And it will help you move forward."

A group without a process can't innovate. A group with a process, combined with spirit and competence, can change the world. Just ask Margaret Mead.

HOW TO MASTER THIS I-SKILL

To become a standout collaborator, you must always have an eye on the bigger picture. You must conduct yourself with an eye to reputation, results, and residuals.

When you work intensely with other people in small collaborative teams, they come to know you—your personality, your character, your strengths, and your weaknesses. When you've completed a major collaborative task or project and you're more respected because of it, you'll know that you are on your way to mastering this important skill. If you're asked more and more often to join other teams and are increasingly complimented as a fun person to be around, you'll know that you're on the road to seeking mastery of self, which always precedes mastery of this I-Skill.

And now you're ready to tackle the final, essential, capstone I-Skill of them all: the ability to persuade others to buy your ideas.

$I-Skill \#7$

Build the Buy-In for New Ideas

Tools and Techniques for Selling Your Innovations to Co-Workers, the Boss, and the End Customer

I'm standing atop the Sydney Harbour Bridge in Australia enjoying the most spectacular scene imaginable. It's breezy up here and you can see for miles in all directions. Off to my right, the world-famous Sydney Opera House beckons ships entering Darling Harbour, as sailboats and ferries glide across the cerulean waters. Behind me stand the steel and glass skyscrapers of downtown Sydney. A hundred meters below, cars look like children's toys as they zip back and forth on the roadway, and a passenger train lumbers across.

Don't get the idea what I'm doing is risky. I'm with a small group of tourists from all over the world, and we're all strapped in at the waistband with safety cables that attach to a master line. To come up here, first you must empty your pockets into a locker, don a special nylon jumpsuit and hat, pass through a metal detector, take a Breathalyzer test, submit to being patted down, and attend a briefing. This is a thriving business, and 2 million people have been up here before me. Our guide, a wisecracking young fellow from Melbourne, tells us how this concession came to be.

An entrepreneur named Paul Cave, looking for something memorable to do for a World Congress of the Young Presidents Organization, got special permission to organize a group climb. Everybody had so much fun that Cave hatched an idea: He decided that more people deserved to experience the breathtaking monument and the spectacular views from atop the Sydney Harbour Bridge.

It took a grueling nine years of overcoming bureaucratic objections and political hurdles before Cave's vision was transformed into BridgeClimb. What if a tourist lost his footing? Hence the safety cable system. What if somebody drops their car keys on the cars below? Hence the empty pockets and the jumpsuit. What if somebody is inebriated? Hence the Breathalyzer.

Selling new ideas, as Cave's story aptly demonstrates, has always been about surmounting obstacles, overcoming objections, and gaining commitment for change. Everyone agrees in principle that organizations need to innovate. Everyone agrees they must become more agile to compete in today's hypercompetitive world. But on the road between this general agreement and your specific new idea being adopted, there are bound to be speed bumps galore and more than a few potholes to slow you down or block your progress.

Innovating successfully in the era of disruption requires that you master a multifaceted set of persuasion techniques that I call building the buy-in, and that's our final I-Skill.

WHAT BUILDING THE BUY-IN ENTAILS

In this chapter, we'll focus primarily on building the buy-in for ideas and new initiatives that will have a major impact—ideas that improve processes, cut costs, and produce new products and services that grow revenue. But make no mistake: the I-Skill you are developing comes in handy in more mundane, everyday situations as well. For example, let's say that as a result of reading about the importance of taking a Doug Day, you decide that's exactly what you need to do. Chances are you need to get approval to take off on a weekday and not show up for work. Alas, you must build the buy-in with your boss and with your team perhaps to act on this idea. So as you consider the ideas in this chapter, keep in mind that you can use this skill not just for the big ideas but for smaller ones too.

Remember Jonathan A., the first-year accountant we met in Chapter 2? He doesn't need to build the buy-in to collect ideas to speed up how he completes his work. The only objections he needs to overcome are personal assumptions: I'm too busy falling behind to seek out new methods. They don't want me to find new ways to accomplish my work in less time and without my having to "eat hours."

Sue Kinnick, the VA Hospital nurse, had to persuade her colleagues and teammates at the Topeka, Kansas, hospital where she worked. And together, she and her team built a strong case for senior management, and later, for adoption by the entire VA hospital system, to begin bar-coding medications. And on it goes.

For bigger ideas, you and your team need buy-in from suppliers, alliance partners, distributors, channel partners, and assorted other stakeholders who wield the power to kiss or kill the idea. And of course, the ultimate test is whether you can build the buy-in with paying customers as well. This means gaining acceptance for the product or service or solution in the marketplace. It means decision makers approve of it. Purchasing directors purchase it. Customers buy it. In the final analysis, an innovation is not really an innovation until it produces top- and bottom-line revenue growth.

Internally in an organization, this requires that you be successful in getting the idea approved, funded, staffed, implemented, and accepted. Your team needs buy-in from decision makers in the organization. Your team needs continued support from senior managers in the organization to support the idea over time.

8 WAYS TO BUILD THE BUY-IN FOR NEW IDEAS

Are you ready to master this final I-Skill necessary for successful innovation? If so, here are eight powerful methods for building the buy-in for your ideas.

1. Do your homework.
2. Let others think it was their idea.
3. Customize your communication style.
4. Make it safe for buyers to say yes.
5. Focus on benefits and overcoming resistance.
6. Use the power of stories.
7. Cross boundaries to build support for your idea.
8. Be persistent.

1. Do Your Homework

Does the new idea add value? Is it doable? Once you've done your homework and have isolated the benefits, you're ready to get feedback on your idea. Start with friends, teammates, mentors, and other people whom you trust to be forthright but sympathetic.

The more others can feel, taste, touch, and "see" the idea represented, as if it's already a reality and operational, the greater your selling success. So make a sketch, create slides. Do anything that is visual and provides a common reference point. Effective communication is half the battle. People don't like to admit that they "don't get it," that they don't understand your idea, that it's too complicated. But as every evangelist knows, if people don't understand, they don't buy.

Help people to see what your vision could be.

Any proposed change must concern itself with the issue of customer acceptance. How long does it take all your various customers, channel partners, gatekeepers, and end users to integrate your new products and services, to amortize the costs, or to find the time to learn how to use your new ideas? And what can you do at the beginning of the pipeline to accelerate the customer's ability to derive value from your ideas at the end of the pipeline?

2. Let Others Think it Was Their Idea

Nelnet innovation champion Evan Roth once said to me that "the key is to position things so that it doesn't appear as 'my idea' but a joint idea or even their idea. It is easier to sell someone his or her own idea and not be so concerned with taking credit. Ultimately, the business unit has to execute on the idea anyway. For me, the reward is seeing the initiative implemented, regardless of whose idea it was."

One worker told me: "The best technique I've used is to build relationships with others based on past experiences or by building credibility in my recommendations. Fact-based logic is the best approach to take; however, it isn't enough to sell the idea. Persistence is another key trait. Also, obtaining alignment with key influencers is critical to pushing an idea up the chain within my division."

Here, from one of my surveys, is a comment to reflect on: "Agree to yourself not to force yourself and your ideas. Friction comes from one thing: lack of respect. Don't be intrusive or overbearing. It's not all about you, you're not always right. If you find someone avoiding you, it's probably for a reason of your own making. You haven't respected someone in some way, now they want nothing to do with you, and the friction has begun."

Innovators share credit.

3. Customize Your Communication Style

How you "sell" an idea depends to a great extent on whom you're selling it to. If you're making a pitch to senior management about an idea management funding committee, that's a different sales job than presenting an idea to your team. If you're presenting an idea to the board of directors, that's different from presenting to your colleagues. Effective evangelists find out as much as they can about the thinking styles of those they are pitching. If you deal with a mix of people, such as marketing, sales, human resources, finance, information technology (IT), and other specializations, you'll need to incorporate various devices to satisfy the members of each group.

Think about the innovation style of the person or persons you'll be presenting your idea to. Are they visioning, exploring, modifying, or experimenting? Do they tend to be more comfortable changing the system or perfecting the system? Analytical persons need the data and numbers that make the case for your idea. If your audience is more big picture–oriented, don't bog them down with details. They realize all these things have to be worked out. Instead, make sure you demonstrate how the idea is in alignment with the firm's growth targets and how it advances the firm's goals. Use their hot-button words. No matter who your audience is, be crystal clear in the way you describe your idea, and in the way you build your case, so that nobody gets left behind in the complexity.

Innovators use familiar language.

4. Make It Safe for Buyers to Say Yes

Your new idea says, "There's got to be a better way and this is it. The way we're solving this problem today is not as

173

good as the way we could be solving the problem." But it also suggests that people trade the security and safety of the present way for a new way that has potential dangers. It asks that they take a risk, a leap from the known to the unknown. That's why it's essential to put yourself in the other person's shoes and ease his or her discomfort by minimizing the risks to make it safe for the idea buyer to say yes.

One way to do this is by safe experimentation. How can you make reversibility a way to get people to try out your idea? The age-old "money back guarantee" is one proven way. Reassure people that they can easily go back to the old way of doing things if they ultimately don't like the new method you are proposing. This lowers their resistance. It is hoped that the results they achieve will more than make up for the costs of shifting to your innovative way of doing things, and they won't want to go back.

5. Focus on Benefits and Overcoming Resistance

Benefits are what every salesperson learns to focus on by addressing the issue of "what's in it for me?" That means explaining not how the idea will work or its features but what it will do for those for whom it is planned to bring added value. Will it create additional customer satisfaction because it provides greater speed or convenience? Will it reduce costs to your organization? Will it raise employee morale or make the workplace a little more fun? Will it increase safety or aid efficiency?

No matter how obvious the benefits, few ideas sell themselves. You'll experience resistance, and sometimes you may not be able to pinpoint where it's coming from, either

174

internally or externally. You'll encounter problems that you never could have foreseen. The market will react totally apart from what you or anyone on your team expected. So the experienced innovator knows to expect the unexpected and anticipate continuing to overcome objections, sell skeptics, and deal with the unexpected.

Marketing an innovation, both internally and externally, depends on convincing people to adopt a new idea. Implicitly, it demands that they accept change. Adoption of your idea requires a learning process to get up and running. It is undertaken either because it is required of the individual—by the person you report to, say—or undertaken voluntarily. The latter is based on a complex set of beliefs, feelings, and motivations—from the "desire to impress others" to "not wanting to appear behind the times."

Such resistance is to be expected with truly new ways of doing things, no matter what the promised benefits and no matter the promise of the proffered value proposition.

Innovators realize they will face resistance. And they focus on selling the benefits of making the change to win acceptance.

The growing reality is that there are simply too many ideas and too many initiatives—albeit, incremental improvements and line extensions—chasing the finite resources and a finite ability to adopt them all.

Innovations must be timed for optimal acceptance.

6. Use the Power of Stories
When you tell stories, it sets off the imaginations of people and they take your ideas wherever they will as fuel for their

own creative fires. They love you for helping to stimulate them in this way. It's the thing that keeps it exciting for me on the lecture trail. An executive came up to me after one of my talks and said, "I was with you about 80 percent of the time, and I was so taken by what you were saying because you were putting words to things that I have thought about in the back of my mind but never took the time to write down. But," he paused for a breath, "I've got to tell you the other 20 percent of the time I wasn't listening to you because I was writing so fast to capture the ideas that were suddenly flooding my mind. I'm leaving here [pointing to his notepad] with an idea that I'm definitely going to act on."

7. Cross Boundaries to Build Support for Your Idea

I asked Best Buy's Jennifer Rock about the obstacles she had to overcome to gain support for a new department. "What you are doing strikes me as traditionally the turf of Human Resources. How did you navigate around that? Did you get pushback from HR?"

"I think it's all about the relationships that you form," she replied. "It's making sure our HR partners are onboard with what we are doing and trying." In other words, where some might see problems, Jen spoke soothingly about mutually beneficial opportunities. Where some see turf battles, Jennifer sees the chance to partner, the need to communicate, and the process of creating win-win opportunities for all.

Being a problem solver is an integral part of being an effective innovator—especially if the problem involves people and especially if the people involved are from different silos in an organization. (The silos I speak of here could be a business unit, a department, a division, a region, or a territory.)

We humans tend to be loyal to our silo, and since we produce a certain output—IT solutions or payroll solutions, say—a common language develops. Leaders of silos build morale quite often by reinforcing the shared values and common assumptions that define the subgroup. The silo's interests are not necessarily the same as those of other silos or other power centers in the organization. So what is often necessary for innovation to take place to unite differing silos, to build trust, and to engender communication between silos? Whose job is this? Who are the bridge-builders and the few in any organization with the motivation and the skills to do what is necessary? Why, the innovators of course.

8. Be Persistent

The 3M team responsible for launching Post-it Notes was growing desperate. Senior management was threatening to kill the product as a loser. The product was in a few stores, but nobody was buying it. Getting retailers to stock the product was proving to be nearly impossible. Retailers didn't understand the product, their customers weren't clamoring for it, and who needed these silly little stacks of paper when you could just use scratch paper? What to do?

"Richmond," someone suggested. And so several members of the 3M team took suitcases of the little sticky pads to the business district of Richmond, Virginia, and handed them out to passersby. It was a turning point. People started sticking them everywhere, finding uses, and they began asking for them at retail stores. The rest is innovation history.

Post-it Notes have brought additional billions to 3M's top and bottom lines and stands as an icon of this final ingredient of the innovation process.

Discovery and invention of a new product or service are not nearly enough. To derive growth from innovation, you have to build the buy-in for your idea, sometimes one customer at a time. You have to go out and knock on doors, and find people who can use your product. These days, as computer mouse inventor Douglas Engelbart put it, the biggest challenge isn't how to innovate a better mousetrap; it's how to get people to adopt your better mousetrap.

People don't know they need your innovation until they try it.

HOW TO MASTER THIS I-SKILL

Successfully selling new ideas is the essential, capstone skill of innovation-adept leaders. In the public's imagination, selling often gets confused with hucksterism, manipulation, politicians, pushy salespeople, and unsavory practices. But as every successful innovator knows, nothing happens until the sale is made.

As you ponder the suggestions and techniques in this chapter, consider this: Try to anchor your idea in as many places inside the company, and with as many customers that are important outside the company, as possible.

Ask yourself:

- Is the idea aligned with my sphere of influence, track record for execution, and overall reputation?
- Is the timing right to pursue this idea at this time?

- Have I sown plenty of seeds and educated influential people on the merits of making this change?
- Who has actually used this idea and what have the results been?
- What information or expertise do I need to obtain to accomplish this goal?

Mark Twain once said, "I'm all for progress. It's change that I don't like." And so it is with most of humanity. And so it is with pursuing new ways of doing things. Learn to enjoy the journey from idea to implementation because your idea quest will almost always end up someplace you didn't quite expect. The important thing isn't so much whether you and your team scored a home run but that you enhanced your reputation for being a key player and for earnestly trying. For having taken a risk rather than sitting on the sidelines and watching. For having come up with an idea that was strong, well supported, and timely.

A FINAL WORD

As I put this book to bed and send it off for publication, I think about the choice we first discussed in Chapter 1.

It's the choice to continue to do what you do in the way you've always done it—and hope that the winds of disruptive change somehow blow over and leave you unaffected.

Because you've read this far, I know you're a person who wants to make a different choice. That choice involves seizing upon the message of this book and taking charge of developing and using your I-Skills to navigate your career in a completely different direction. Good luck and much success in your journey.

Notes

CHAPTER 1

"I've got a lot of autonomy in my job . . ." is from interview with the author. Note: many of the 43 people interviewed for this book were speaking without authorization from corporate communications, so asked that their names not be used.

CHAPTER 2

"We look for adaptability and flexibility . . .": Anne Mulcahy's comments are from "The Keeper of the Tapping Pencil," an interview with the Xerox CEO by Adam Bryant, *New York Times*, March 21, 2009.

"With the cost of employing people going through the roof . . ." Brent Gow's comments are from an interview with the author.

"As a first year auditor, I am not encouraged to be innovative . . ." Jonathan A's comments are from an interview with Ariel Cohen, researcher for this book.

The late Sue Kimmick's story is from an interview with Chris Tucker, an associate of the nurse, by the author.

CHAPTER 3

"I think the first thing they'd probably say is . . ." Lisa Peters'
comments are from interview with the author.

"At Whirlpool we solve people's chores . . ." Moises Norena's
comments are from an interview with the author.

Just 21 percent of the employees surveyed are engaged in
their work. This statistic is from "Study Finds Significant
'Engagement Gap' Among Global Workforce," Towers
Perrin Study published October 22, 2007.

The Innovation Styles Inventory was created by William
Miller. For more information see: innovationstyles.com

I-SKILL #1: EMBRACE THE OPPORTUNITY MINDSET

"I couldn't get it out of my mind," Donald Schoendorfer's
comment is from the charity's web site. See: Freewheel
chairmission.org

"Customers call us all day long and sometimes they are
unhappy . . ." professor Alan Robinson's comments
are from Corporate Creativity, by Alan Robinson and
Sam Stern (Berrett-Koehler, 1997).

Clayton Christensen's book The Innovator's Dilemma, was
published in 1997 by Harvard Business Press.

"I hold laziness to be an engineer's highest virtue . . ." Cox
Communications' Matt Carothers' comments are from an
interview with the author.

"My background was in sales . . ." Xerox's Tom Dolan's
comments are from an interview with the author.

I-SKILL #2: BECOME AN ASSUMPTION ASSAULTER

"People have a lot of choices of where they'll stay. . . ."

"Victor's" comments are from interviews with the author.

"When people are faced with a majority of others who agree on a particular attitude . . ." Charlan Nemeth's observation's are from her article "Managing Innovation: When Less is More," *California Management Review*, Fall, 1997.

Juliet Shorr's research in working hours is from her book, The Overworked American, Basic Books, 1992 page 29.

Every day, the average user sends 34 emails and receives 99 email according to research from the Radicati Group, which notes that corporate email traffic continues its dramatic rise worldwide.

"The people who don't believe they've been blessed with creativity. . . ." David Campbell's comments are from an interview with the author.

"Mostly you go down paths that go nowhere . . ." Lee Clow's comments are from an interview with the author.

"You can be really innovative but if the organization you work for doesn't change . . ." Nancy Snyder's observations are from an interview with the author.

"The creativity I'm talking about is different from problem-solving . . ." Michael Ray's comments are from his book Creativity in Business, by Michael Ray and Rochelle Myers, Doubleday, 1986.

I-SKILL #3: A PASSION FOR THE END CUSTOMER

"Our success, as with any retailer, boils down to the interaction between one customer and one employee . . ." Jennifer Rock's comments are from an interview with the author.

I-SKILL #4: THINK AHEAD OF THE CURVE

"Thinking what your opponent will do three moves out is good discipline . . ." Filippo Passerini's comments are from an interview with the author.

"My network is where I get some of my best ideas . . ." John Draper's comments are from an interview with the author.

"I would recommend developing an expertise network . . ." Christopher Rollyson's comments are from an interview with the author.

"Our ability to interpret text, to make the rich mental connections that form when we read deeply . . ." Nicholas Carr's ideas are from his article "Is Google Making Us Stupid?" Atlantic Monthly, July/August 2008.

"Vision is just a lot of grinding it out information gathering . . ." Frederick Smith's comments are from a personal interview with the author.

I-SKILL #5: FORTIFY YOUR IDEA FACTORY

"Once a month I schedule what I refer to as a Doug Day . . ." Doug Greene's comments are from an interview with the author, first reported in the book, *Winning the Innovation Game*, published by Baker House Books, 1986.

"I was eager to transfer because of the opportunity . . ." Justin Welke's comments are from "the Best Places to Launch a Career," Bloomberg BusinessWeek, September 14, 2009 every day, the average user sends 34 emails and receives 99 emails.

"Multitaskers were just lousy at everything . . ." Clifford Nass' comments are from "The Mediocre Multitasker," by Ruth Pennebaker, New York Times, August 30, 2009.

One in five executives take along laptops on vacation: from "One in Five Take Laptops Along on Vacation," by Alan Fram, Santa Barbara News Press, June 2, 2007.

I-SKILL #6: BECOME A STANDOUT COLLABORATOR

"I've got pretty good eyesight . . ." Whirlpool CEO Dave Whitwam's comments are from "A Chat With Dave Whitwam," BusinessWeek, September 21, 2000.

"Figure out how to work in teams . . ." Nancy Snyder's comments are from an interview with the author.

"You can have a great person who doesn't really work well on a team . . ." Will Wright's comment is from "Are You a Solvent, or the Glue?" an interview conducted by Adam Bryant, New York Times, June 14, 2009.

I-SKILL #7: BUILD THE BUY-IN FOR NEW IDEAS

"the key is to position things so that it doesn't appear to be my idea . . ." Evan Roth's comments are from an interview with the author.

Acknowledgments

I would like to extend my thanks and sincere appreciation to the many people who helped make this book possible.

- To my wife, Carolyn McQuay, whose love, support, and companionship make my life complete.
- To Robert Jacobson, who was an early supporter of this project and who introduced us to a number of the folks you'll read about in these pages. Thank you, Bob, for your generous, giving nature and for the stimulating conversations we had.
- To Jonathan Vejar, Blair Miller, and Tom Mulhern, for the phrase "the innovator's mindset, skillset, and toolset," which is the essence of what this book is about.
- To all the managers, CEOs, and individual contributors we interviewed for this book. Many, it turned out, were reluctant about having their names in print for fear of grandstanding or taking undue credit.
- To my crackerjack research team, mostly composed of graduate and undergraduate students from the University of California, Santa Barbara: Erica Johnson, Ariel Cohen, Samantha Lutz, Jeff Sloan, Cara Rose Tucker, Jennifer Wilson, and Margaret Retsch.

Acknowledgments

- To the talented Susan Suffes, who helped shape the initial manuscript into something resembling prose.

- To the many people who read and commented on the manuscript, including Rebecca Winter, Karen Tucker, Peter Chee, Rinaldo Brutoco, Katherine Armstrong, Danielle Scott, Dave Wood, Mike McNair, Jeevan Sivasubramaniam, and Steve Piersanti.

- And finally, to the agent James Levine, for introducing me to the world-class team at John Wiley & Sons, especially senior editor Richard Narramore and senior production editor Deborah Schindlar. Thank you for helping to make this book the best it can be.

About the Author

Robert B. Tucker is president of The Innovation Resource Consulting Group. He is one of the most in-demand innovation speakers, workshop leaders, and consultants in the world today. He coaches rank-and-file employees, managers, senior executives, and entire organizations in achieving higher rates of productivity and growth through innovation mastery.

Formerly an adjunct professor at the University of California, Los Angeles, Tucker took a pioneering look at the success traits of leading innovators, and the results became the book *Winning the Innovation Game* in 1986. His 1992 international bestseller *Managing the Future: 10 Driving Forces of Change* examined the deep-seated drivers of consumer and societal behavior. *Driving Growth Through Innovation*, published in 2002, reported on 23 "innovation vanguard firms" that were in the forefront of establishing systematic, all-enterprise approaches to innovation.

Clients range from Global 500 companies to national and international trade associations and nonprofit and governmental organizations. Tucker has been a consultant to Taiwan's Economic Development Ministry, the Japan

About the Author

Marketing Association, and Easter Seals Society. He has shared his empowering tools and techniques with groups throughout North America and in 35 countries.

As one of the thought leaders in the growing Innovation Movement, Tucker is a frequent blogger and contributor to business periodicals such as *Journal of Business Strategy, Harvard Management Update*, and *Strategy & Leadership*. His quarterly *Tucker on Innovation* is read by thousands of devotees around the world. A frequent talk show host himself at conferences and corporate convocations, he has appeared on PBS, CBS Radio, and India's Network 18; he was also a featured guest on the CNBC series *The Business of Innovation*, hosted by Maria Bartiromo.

To communicate with Robert Tucker, to schedule a speaking engagement, or for more information about his books, online learning programs, and audio and video recordings, visit www.innovationresource.com or contact:

The Innovation Resource
100 North Hope Avenue, Suite 19
Santa Barbara, California 93110
United States of America
Tel: (805) 682-1012
E-mail: info@innovationresource.com

Index

Index

Index

Index